ESP

How I Developed My Sixth Sense And So Can You

**Other books by
Stephen Hawley Martin**

*The True Holy Grail
The Secret You Can Use to Create the Life You Want*

*How Science Reveals God
What Every Thinking Person Must Know*

*The Truth about Life
And How to Make Yours the Best of All*

*Edgar Cayce,
The Meaning of Life and What to Do About It*

*A Witch in the Family
The Salem Witch Trials Re-examined
In Light of New Evidence*

*Actual Magic
The Secret to Manifesting Your Desires*

*Afterlife, The Whole Truth
Life After Death Books I & II*

*Can Christianity Make a Comeback?
Yes, and Here's How*

*The Search for Nina Fletcher
You Won't Put This Book Down Until She Is Found*

*The Secret of Life
An Adventure Out of Body, Into Mind*

*Death in Advertising
A Whodunit*

ESP

How I Developed My Sixth Sense And So Can You

By

Stephen Hawley Martin

WWW.OAKLEAPRESS.COM

ESP: How I Developed My Sixth Sense and So Can You © 2023 by Stephen Hawley Martin. All rights reserved. No part of this book may be used or reproduced in any manner whatsoever without written permission except in the case of brief quotations embodied in critical articles and reviews. For information visit:

www.oakleapress.com

CONTENTS

Chapter One: Journey to Revelation 7

Chapter Two: The Reading 28

Chapter Three: Develop the Right Mindset 57

Chapter Four: Entrain Your Mind 80

Chapter Five: Ask and Expect to Receive 101

Chapter Six: Keys that Unlock Intuition 111

About the Author and His Other Books 130

"If you listen to your inner voice, your inner wisdom—which is far greater than anybody else's as far as you are concerned—you will not go wrong and you will know what to do with your life."

—Elisabeth Kübler-Ross [1926-2004]

Chapter One
Journey to Revelation

The year was 2002. The beep of the alarm sounded. As though connected to someone else's arm, my hand flopped toward my bedside table and pushed down the off switch. I rolled onto my back. Shadows of tree limbs crisscrossed a square of light on the ceiling. I was tempted to shut my eyes just for a moment.

Better not, I thought. Time to get moving.

As quietly as possible, I rolled out of bed and groped my way through inky shadows. My hand found a rheostat knob and I turned it until there was just enough light to shave by. No sense waking the house, especially my two and a half year old son in the next room who'd want me to fix him a waffle. It would be impossible to make him understand that it was still practically the middle of the night, that he needed to go back to bed, and that I had a plane to catch.

The warm spray of the shower engulfed me and washed sleep from my eyes. Thoughts of the trip ahead played in my mind. This would be my second visit to the School of Metaphysics, the first having been a couple of months before. I'd gone then at the invitation of Dr. Laurel Clark, a faculty member and editor of *Thresholds,* the School's quarterly magazine, which had published some of my articles. That weekend retreat had been intended to help participants develop their intuitive abilities. I'd been impressed by what I'd experienced, but what had most captured my attention were the intuitive readings given by Doctors Barbara and Dan Condron. They used the same technique the well-known twentieth-century psychic Edgar Cayce [1877-1945] had employed for decades before his death. I had no idea this sort of thing was being done.

I rubbed soap onto a wet washcloth and thought of the biography of Cayce I'd read recently. The majority of his readings had involved health issues that had baffled medical doctors. Cayce would put himself into a hypnotic trance and answer questions. Not only did Cayce accurately diagnose problems and give detailed and specific instructions for curing them, he also provided insights into the root cause that had led to a condition. Sometimes the illness had its origin in a previous life.

Like Barbara Condron and other School of Metaphysics readers, Cayce did not consciously remember what he'd said while in a trance. To find out he had to read a transcription. A life-long Presbyterian, he'd had difficulty accepting reincarnation as a real phenomenon when an account had first appeared in his readings. Nevertheless, the information had proven so helpful in allowing someone to put issues behind her and to begin to lead a productive life he begrudgingly accepted it might be possible. Following this first episode, many of those requesting readings from Cayce were found to have issues from past lives that needed to be resolved.

I grabbed a bottle of shampoo and squeezed some into my hand.

Today, an open-minded individual familiar with the evidence would have difficulty refuting reincarnation. For example, Ian Stevenson [1918-2007], who had been the Carlson Professor of Psychiatry and Director of the Division of Perceptual Studies at the University of Virginia School of Medicine, collected over 2,500 cases of children who remembered past-lives and was able to verify about half of them based on recalled information that checked out. Detailed reports of many have been published. Specific information was matched with the former identity, including family, names, residence, and manner of death. Professor Stevenson has found that birthmarks and other physiological manifestations often relate to experiences of the remembered past life, particularly when violent death is involved.

After the shower I dressed in the dark, grabbed my suitcase which I'd packed the night before, and descended the steps. I checked my watch. No time for breakfast.

Outside, the air was balmy and slightly humid. Crickets, cicadas and tree frogs created babble as old as Mother Earth.

I paused by the door to my Jeep in awe of the abundance of creatures that must inhabit the tall trees and thickets around my house. It occurred to me that I was hearing a loud and clear symphony being performed by the Source of All Life.

A whippoorwill let out a call, and I snapped out of my reverie. It was time to climb behind the wheel of my Jeep and to point it toward the airport.

Readings performed during the intuition retreat weekend had determined what type of intuition each participant favored. For example, some people saw visions or symbols. This is called clairvoyance. Others heard voices. My preference was psychometry, which involves focusing on a person, place or thing to bring my conscious and subconscious minds in line with one another. The readings also had explored how each person might further develop or hone abilities. What I learned about myself had seemed so accurate, and had proven so helpful, that I decided to have a past-life reading done as well.

Over the years I've become acquainted with several past-life therapists. At least two have offered to regress me or in some other way help me remember past lives. I've always resisted because it didn't seem necessary for me to know, or perhaps more truthfully, I thought it might be upsetting to find out. But I'd reached a crossroads in my life and was searching for direction. So, as soon as I returned from the weekend on intuition, I filled out a form printed from the School of Metaphysics web site and mailed it along with a check.

You may be wondering how these readings are done. Two individuals are involved, a conductor and a reader. The conductor guides the reader into a hypnotic state and instructs her to relate a past life that is significant to the subject's present life and current situation. These sessions are recorded and the recording is sent to the subject. I suppose I was expecting to hear of a past life as a Druid or perhaps an Egyptian priest since so much of my current situation and writings have to do with things metaphysical. But this wasn't the case.

As I turned on to Interstate 64 toward the airport, I

thought about that past life reading. Supposedly, I was born into a politically and militarily active family in Russia in the 19th century. Traditionally, the men of this family became military officers and afterwards many accepted influential positions in the government. Since this was also seen as my destiny, my elders began while I was still quite young to coach me in this regard.

I was apparently a willing and able student. At puberty I entered the military and quickly became something of a star, rapidly rising to a relatively high level of command. War broke out. From other information included in the reading, I'm guessing Napoleon's army invaded Russia. I led my men into combat to defend the motherland. During the ensuing battle, a strategically placed cannon became jammed. I rushed to fix it. When it finally fired, I was killed by the blast.

I was 23 years old.

The airport was up ahead. I took my foot off the accelerator.

According to the reading, much mourning took place throughout the land. The implication was that I was well known and people thought I was headed for greatness when my life was cut short. Apparently, this is why I'm a restless person today who is constantly pursuing goals that even if accomplished may not contribute in any meaningful way to my personal evolution. I was told that I needed to look inward, and to ask my Higher Self who I wanted to be and what I wanted to accomplish in this life. The reading concluded with the words, "For we see that this one has a mission, an assignment to accomplish, which is leadership."

My heart had sunk when I heard this. This was supposed to be a past life that was relevant to my current situation. Not since I was a child, however, could I remember longing for a position of leadership. Frankly, as president of my own company, and later as chief administrative officer of a much larger firm, I'd had my fill of it. Being the leader meant taking on everyone else's problems, and I no longer gave a darn if someone longed for a wooden trash can or an office with a view. What I wanted at this point in life was to sit at my keyboard and create. I wanted to be a full-time novelist. This being the case, how could my mission have anything to do with leadership?

The idea of "an assignment" also had me puzzled. The terminology seemed to indicate I had a specific task to perform.

I came to a stop at the airport parking lot ticket dispenser. It seemed as though I'd just left my driveway. I started off, pushed in the clutch and pulled the shift lever into second as I glided past a sign that said the first level of parking was filled.

Leadership. Leadership of what?

I hoped to heaven the coming weekend would provide the answers. I was coming up on a crossroads in life and needed to know which way to turn, and I'd been assured that at this weekend retreat I would learn my Dharma.

My fight on American Airlines out of Richmond headed to Dallas where I had to wait a couple of hours before boarding a commuter flight. Noon came and went. It was almost three o'clock before the twin-engine jet prop lumbered in for a landing at Springfield, Missouri. I peered out of my window. Having left lush vegetation in Virginia, the trees and brush rising up from below seemed slightly stunted and the leaves appeared to be covered with a film of dust as though the earth needed a long, cool drink. The open spaces were a shade between yellow and beige.

A blast of warm air greeted me as I left the airport through automatic doors, my Thrifty Rental Car contract in hand. I hoisted my suitcase and wiped sweat from the back of my neck with a red bandana pulled from my back pocket. Fortunately, the lot was not far from the terminal, the car was where it was supposed to be, and the air conditioning worked.

The hand-drawn map that had been sent to me indicated the first leg of my journey would be a short stint on Interstate 44, then I'd need to turn north onto a secondary road and continue for what appeared to be forty or fifty miles.

As I cruised along it occurred to me that this land not only seemed dryer than Virginia, it also seemed higher. Or maybe the clouds were lower. I realized, of course; that I was headed into the Ozark Mountains, but aside from rock outcroppings and occasional stone-faced cliffs, this area could pass for rolling Piedmont countryside in Virginia during a drought.

After a while I arrived in the town of Buffalo, seat of government of Dallas County, Missouri. I took a right and a left. Ten or fifteen minutes and a few turns later I reached Windyville, a crossroads and three or four buildings of Tom Sawyer vintage.

I stopped and checked the map, then made a left onto a gravel road where, 1.8 miles later, would be the front gate to the School of Metaphysics.

I could see dust flying in the rearview mirror. I slowed down, hung a left through the gate, and pointed the car toward

ESP

the large white building that I knew to house classrooms and a dining facility. A car came toward me from that direction. It slowed and stopped. I stepped on the brake. Dr. Laurel rolled down her window, a petite woman, slim, with a kind face and a gentle smile.

"Welcome," she said.

"Thanks. Where're you headed?"

"Just over to the ranch. Christine's at the School. She'll bring you in a little while." She smiled and gave a little wave.

"See you then."

I nodded, pressed on the gas and marveled at this place. It was in such a sparsely populated area, almost in the geographic center of the United States. Branches of the School are located in cities throughout the Midwest, and correspondence courses are given to people located all over the world; yet only a few dozen students attend full time at this, the Windyville campus, even though it encompasses more than a thousand acres.

I parked in a line of cars and walked fifteen or twenty yards to the building. Every living thing looked like it could use some water except the vegetable garden, which was off to my left. Some sort of irrigation system must have been keeping it green.

ESP

Thirty yards to the right was a large penned area for chickens. I could see some milling around. Eggs, milk and milk products such as butter and cheese, as well as beef, pork, vegetables—all were raised and consumed by the students and faculty.

I went through the door, descended steps and stepped over a dog that was sprawled on the cement floor. No doubt he'd chosen the coolest spot.

Sure enough, there was Christine—blond, medium height. Last time I'd been here she'd given me a ride from the airport. Her smile seemed to indicate she knew more than she let on. Her eyes revealed a soul at peace. An old soul. She opened her arms for a hug, and then led me inside.

We walked past the long table where meals were served.

Dr. Barbara, round-faced, cheery, was with some students in the kitchen preparing the evening meal. They all stopped what they were doing and welcomed me. When I learned we were having clam chowder for dinner, I chuckled and wondered aloud how it was possible to raise clams in Missouri.

The weekend retreats that are held by the School take place about a half mile away from the main building at what's known as the Moon Valley Ranch, a charming hundred year old clapboard house with large rooms and a covered front porch made of stone. The ten attendees of the Dharma weekend, plus Dr. Laurel, who was to lead the session, and Christine, who was to help her, would sleep at the ranch. After Friday night's clam chowder in a bread bowl, we'd take meals there as well. Between eating and sleeping we would learn about and discuss our particular reasons for incarnating this time around.

Christine drove me there. I entered the back door and took off my shoes, recalling that shoes weren't allowed inside. This time I'd brought my bedroom slippers.

Perhaps my reputation for snoring had gotten out the last time I was here, or maybe I was just lucky, or maybe the School wanted to be extra nice to me for some reason, but no matter the motive, I was assigned the only private room.

About seven o'clock Friday evening, the attendees, Dr. Laurel, Christine, and Dr. Dan, who is chancellor of the School, all gathered in the living room. We sat in a large circle and each of us told the others about ourselves.

Dr. Dan, who was tall and slim but with the beginnings of a tummy that made me think of the Buddha, sat in a straight back dining room chair with his legs crossed at the ankles. He announced that he would be attending the session as one of us so that he'd know firsthand what this weekend was like. Two other attendees were chiropractors, one male and the other female. Another was the owner of a music store who had just opened an audio and video recording studio. There was an equipment repairman for McDonald's restaurants, a former non commissioned officer who a few months prior had retired from the Air Force, a young man with a graphic arts background who was a partner in an ad agency, a grandmother, an office worker and manager, and myself—a novelist, marketing communications consultant, former ad agency owner and father of four. It seemed fairly certain that by the end of the weekend we'd all know a lot more about one another.

    Then Dr. Laurel shared some background about Dharma. She said it was a Sanskrit word meaning "statute" or "law." Dharma is the law that orders the universe and the essential nature or function of a person or a thing. It is what we have to give or share with others. Even though a person may be good at something, he isn't fulfilling his Dharma if he's primarily after acclaim or money. People who are using their Dharma in the most productive ways tend to be humble, which is not to say they don't or won't receive acclaim. Many do, but they're likely to feel the acclaim isn't really deserved because they so thoroughly enjoy what they do and it comes so naturally to them.

"It is your soul's urge," she continued. "When you are responding to your Dharma, you feel at peace. Someday, after you grow old and look back at life, you will regard the time you spent putting your Dharma to work as the golden years. This is because people who are using their Dharma are passionate about what they do, as though it were a flame burning in them. They lose track of time. They're in the flow. And something else. Each person applies his or her Dharma in a way that is unique as though each of us is one piece of a giant jigsaw puzzle, and we fit together to make up a whole."

"How many different Dharmas are there?" the grandmother asked.

"We don't really know," Laurel said. "We've only been doing Dharma readings for a few years, and this is only our third weekend retreat in as many years. Our students here at the School have a Dharma reading done after they complete their first year."

The retired Air Force noncom raised his hand. "How many readings have been done so far?"

"About seventy," Christine said.

"You must have had some Dharmas repeat," I said. "A few but surprisingly, not many," Christine said.

"And even those that have repeated have manifested differently in different people," Dr. Laurel added. "It's as though there are many shades and hues." She opened a notebook. "Here are some of the Dharmas we've turned up so far:

"Vision: the ability to see probable futures and how things are connected and use this ability in a leadership capacity.

"Synthesis: in this case, identifying needs people have and seeing how to fulfill them with the resources at hand."

"Joy: the ability to bring joy into the lives of others.

"Comprehension: in this case, the ability to see how things fit together. The person who has this was trained as a naturalist and now leads nature walks, explaining to people how nature and the ecosystem work together.

"Compassion: the ability to give comfort to others who may be going through a difficult time.

"Magnetism or charisma: the person who has this uses it to help raise money for charity.

"Others include patience, wholeness, hope, faith, and resilience."

ESP

"What is your Dharma?" I asked.

"Mine is discernment," she said. "It's my nature to want to know the truth and to try to lead others to it as well. Sometimes people feel a little uneasy with me because I ask so many questions. I used to wonder why I felt compelled to do so, and now I know. It's my attempt to thoroughly understand a person's situation and to help them understand it."

The male chiropractor asked, "Are there ways people can determine their Dharma without coming to one of these weekend retreats?"

"Yes," Dr. Laurel said. "One way is for a person to think back to the time before they were seven years old and to remember what they loved to do. When they do so, they need to separate what they liked from what was expected of them. They need to think of all the different activities they loved and try to look for a thread that runs through them.

"It also helps to consider the times in a person's life when they were helping others, having a positive impact, and really felt good about it. Or times when they became lost in an activity and weren't aware of the passing of time."

The conversation continued in this vein, but my thoughts

wandered to my own situation. Perhaps my Dharma was discernment, too. I enjoyed searching for and uncovering the truth. Or maybe it was vision. I seemed to have a knack for seeing all sides of a situation and where it might lead. Or maybe it was comprehension—seeing how various facets and aspects and sides of an issue fit.

My attention was pulled back to Dr. Laurel. She was asking us to write in the journal we'd each been given in order to record the highlights of the weekend. "I want you to answer the question, 'when did you first realize you had a mission?'"

Good question, I thought. When did I?

Then I wrote:

It came to me, not in a flash, but over time. Between adolescence and adulthood I was under the impression life was something a person should try to get through in the most pleasurable way possible. It seemed logical that the main goal should be to make money in order to live well. Eat, drink and be merry for tomorrow you may die. But then I had an out-of-body experience.

This made me ponder life and death and the spiritual side of things. But answers didn't seem to be forthcoming. After a while I

ESP

stopped searching because I came to believe that it was impossible to know.

Then one day I came across a book I couldn't put down. My appetite was whetted, so I took a correspondence course in metaphysics. Over time, I learned how life and the universe works. I'm here this weekend to find out my Dharma so that I can more clearly see the role I should play—my mission in this incarnation.

Next, Dr. Laurel asked us to draw a picture as she passed out crayons, color pencils and paper.

"I want you each to draw a picture of yourself fulfilling your mission."

Wait a minute, I thought. We're here to learn what our mission is.

Hmm, I thought. Maybe that's not exactly right. We're here to learn what our Dharma is, and our Dharma is our essential nature, our soul's urge. That's not the same as a mission—not exactly the same, anyway.

What in the world is my mission? I felt a fluttering of anxiety.

I closed my eyes. Perhaps a vision would come. I silently asked, "What is my mission?"

A sphere of light appeared in my mind's eye. A ladder rose

ESP

into it. Jacob's ladder? I wondered. After a bit, I realized someone was climbing the ladder, and that the person was me. I saw myself turn and offer my hand to someone a rung or two below.

I took some crayons and drew this. I was finished before anyone else. A few minutes passed. Laurel had us sit in a circle and give the rest of the group show and tell.

I held up my drawing. "This is a ladder ascending into the light we call heaven or God—like Jacob's vision of a ladder to heaven. This is me climbing the ladder. You can see that I'm turning to help someone below climb to the next rung. So, my mission is to evolve, to ascend closer to God. But that's only part of my mission. As I make progress, it's my duty as well to help others evolve."

After everyone showed their drawings and talked about them, Christine passed out short white candles in shallow, clear-glass dishes.

Laurel turned out the lights. "I want you to light the candle and concentrate on the flame," she said. "After you've done this for a while, I'll ask you to tell us what you experienced."

I focused on the flame. A halo surrounded it from which

rays shot out. One ray appeared to go farther than the others. It landed on my chest just below my chin and remained there. After a few seconds it seemed that this ray no longer originated from the flame. Rather, it originated in my chest and traveled to the flame as though my inner light now illuminated the flame. I fed the flame and illuminated it. Yet the flame fed my inner light and illuminated me. In a flash of insight I saw this as a metaphor for the circular nature of reality. All is connected. Only one energy exists. There's only one light of which we all are part. I could not recall who said it, but a quotation came to me that expressed the idea that at the end of our journeys we arrive back where we began, but with new and greater understanding. The journey toward God is not straight up a ladder. The path is more like a spiral staircase. When we complete a revolution, we return to the place where we began, but at a higher level than before.

After we each told the others of our experiences with the flame, I looked at my watch. It was almost 9:30. Dr. Laurel said we were done for the evening. At 7:30 the next morning she would lead us in a session of yoga stretching exercises.

She asked if anyone needed a wake up call. I said to please give my door a tap at seven.

ESP

I was in bed by ten, exhausted. Soon, I fell asleep. Then, at about one o'clock, a clap of thunder and a bright flash of light awakened me. Rain had come to that dusty, drought-stricken part of Missouri.

Chapter Two
The Reading

It was still raining when the tap came on the door.

I'd lingered in bed too long because I found that the people in the next room had gotten a jump on me for our shared bathroom. It was almost 7:30 before I emerged with my hair wet and slicked back.

Our yoga exercises were to have been outside, but it was much too wet. We pushed living room furniture against the walls and twelve of us—including Dr. Laurel, Christine and Dr. Dan politely maneuvered for as much room as possible.

Yoga stretching exercises are not my cup of tea. I work out three or more times a week, usually in the form of a long, brisk walk, but I weigh more now than I did when I was a football lineman in college. My body just will not fold itself into the contortions necessary.

Mercifully, that was over within twenty minutes or so. Then we went out the front door onto the porch for a period of guided meditation.

It was gray and cool, rain gently falling. Dr. Laurel had us sit with our backs straight, feet squarely on the floor. We took deep breaths and envisioned the light of our being, first as a glowing ball in our solar plexus. We allowed the ball to grow to encompass our entire bodies, then expand outward to fill the universe.

I felt at peace as I went inward and became aware of the sound of the rain dripping from the leaves of trees, striking the tin roof of the porch. I was reminded of the home I grew up in. This was reinforced by insects singing. The sounds of crickets filled my ears. Birds chimed in as if they were celebrating the rain and the breaking of the drought. A cow mooed in the distance. These were the sounds of Life. A cool, gentle breeze caressed my face. The wind was Life. I was Life.

The Creator was singing through His creation.

My thoughts wandered to the third chapter of the Gospel of John where in conversation with a priest of the ruling class of the Jews, Jesus speaks of being born of "water and the Spirit." (John 3:5) Water represents purification as in Baptism, and the Spirit, as in the Holy Spirit, is God's presence. I was among water and the Spirit on that porch on that ranch that morning in Missouri.

In the same conversation, Jesus said, "I tell you the truth. No one can see the Kingdom of God unless he is born again."

(John 3:3) Jesus is speaking of the shift in consciousness that happens when a person realizes his or her connection to the Divine. Jesus also speaks of wind (John 3:8). He's talking about the air in our lungs, life, or better yet, the Life Force. No one knows where it comes from, or where it goes. But those who are "born again" allow it and the Spirit within to guide them. It is clear he means that the Kingdom of Heaven is not a place. It is a state of mind. He underlined this when he said, "The Kingdom of God does not come with your careful observation, nor will people say, 'Here it is,' or 'There it is,' because the Kingdom of God is within you." (Luke 17:20-21).

Listening to the rain and the insects and the birds, feeling the wind, it occurred to me that this verse might also be translated, "the Kingdom of God is among you," since the Greek word, *entos,* means both "within" and "among." The Kingdom was among our group on that porch that morning. Indeed, the Kingdom of God is "within and among" all of us all of the time. Unfortunately, many are blind to it—they just don't know it's there.

But on that morning in Missouri I could see.

After meditation, we had breakfast. And a good farm breakfast it was. Homegrown eggs, sausage, bacon, scones and homemade butter and jam. Hash brown potatoes on the side. Milk from a real live cow. This wasn't going to help me do the yoga exercises the next morning, but that was almost the last thing on my mind.

At ten o'clock the event I'd been waiting for arrived. We gathered in the living room. A table and chairs were set up for Dr. Dan and Dr. Barbara. Two tape recorders were cued up. Dr. Dan talked Dr. Barbara into a hypnotic trance and the Dharma readings began.

Dr. Dan called on us one at a time, and one at a time we took a seat in front of Dr. Barbara who sat in a large wing chair with her eyes closed.

Several of the attendees preceded me. The grandmother's Dharma was "caring." She had an ability to see what really mattered in a situation and to deliver just the right care. And there was the office manager, for whom it was "devotion." She could become strongly devoted to a person or a cause, but was cautioned to be sure the person or cause was worthy.

Last before me was the male chiropractor. His was synchronicity. He was able to understand how things were connected.

Then it was my turn. I felt butterflies in my stomach as I took my seat.

Dr. Dan turned to Dr. Barbara and said, "You will search the identity of the entity referred to as Stephen Hawley Martin and relate this one's Dharma from the past and past life times in general."

She paused as though waiting for a computer file to boot up, and then said in a kind of sing-song monotone:

"This would most easily be described as an omni-perception. There is a very strong urge within this one to interpret that which this one sees. We see that there is a great deal of reliance upon experience but it is from a more distant place rather than an involvement in it [the experience], and we see that this is in an effort to explore and to develop this perception and to answer the urge for it [perception]. We see that there have been many time periods where this one has been in position to be perceptive. There have been instances where this one has been the eyes and the ears of kings. [There was a pause here and a fumbling for words as if she could not believe what she was now seeing or receiving. Then she continued.] This one spent an entire lifetime living in a crow's nest where the entire endeavor was to be able to hone and develop the

ESP

perception, not only physically but in an otherworldly sense as well. There have been many experiences like these that have been building a complete understanding of perception in its omniscient expression. And we see that this one has the ability to see anything from many different points of view. This one has the capacity, therefore, to be able to recognize a whole picture or a whole image where only a fragment is available. This is a very developed and sharpened intuitive sense where this one is capable of experiencing more in a metaphysical sense than what the physical experience itself would allow. Therefore, it is easy for this one to move beyond the limitations of the physical when this one is entrained with the inner mind and with his Dharma. This is all."

Dr. Dan looked at me. Then he picked up the form I'd filled out earlier and turned it over. I'd written a question in the space provided. He turned to Dr. Barbara, "This one would like to know how he can use his Dharma in the present lifetime to serve others."

Dr. Barbara said:

"This one is doing so in the ways this one is aware of and the ways this one finds appealing. We see that there is much more that could be done in terms of this one's ability to experience it [his Dharma] in the now rather than linking it to the physical forms of expression. The ability for the perception is keen and will be more keenly developed or directed as this one will become more decisive in terms of the intent of the perception. To this point [in time] much of this one's experience has merely been the receiving of this [perception]. There is recognition that this one is driven to experience many different things with many different people in many different ways and forms, and a relishing of this, an appreciation of it that is very deep within this one. There is more, however, that this one can experience with the Dharma by being able to focus the mind upon one point that includes everything. And this [point] is the omnipresence of the perception that this one is capable of in the present time. Therefore, this one would be benefited by beginning to develop inwardly to a greater extent the knowledge of Self to the point of being able to convey this to others. For it is in the conveying of it to others that this one will begin to recognize what this one understands. The interchange is most important for this one, for this is where the greatest opportunity for greater awareness exists. It is in the direct interaction rather than the point of observation. This is all."

Dr. Dan said, "What is the relevance of this one's Dharma to the present lifetime?"

Dr. Barbara answered:

"This one has chosen in the present the conditions whereby there can be the freedom to experience any desire, and many of these have been acted upon, affording this one the availability to experience the omniscience of the perception, and this has brought this one a greater sense of wealth in its true sense. The movement forward would be in the disseminating through interaction of the perception that this one does have. This one has a profound ability as a teacher and a counselor that it would serve this one well to develop."

Dr. Dan asked, "Would it help this one to fulfill his Dharma by being a teacher?"

Dr. Barbara said:

"Yes.

"This is all. . . ."

It had gone by so quickly that I guess I was somewhat in shock.

Omni-perception?

ESP

I'd never heard of omni-perception. My thoughts were spinning.

Dr. Dan was looking at me. "Do you have any more questions?"

"Uh, yes," I said. "What exactly is meant by omni perception?"

Dr. Dan turned to Dr. Barbara. "This one asks what is meant by omni-perception?"

She replied:

"Perception is the mental ability to see, to be able to receive what exists. The omniscience in this is to be able to receive all that exists."

Dr. Dan looked at me. "Anything else?"

"Yes. One more thing," I said. "Did I really spend a lifetime in a crow's nest, or was that some kind of metaphor?"

Dr. Dan turned to her. "Was the 'life in the crow's nest' meant literally? A crow's nest on a ship?"

Dr. Barbara said:

"Yes. This one was at sea for almost the entire lifetime."

Dr. Dan said to her, "Is this all?"

Dr. Barbara said, simply, "Yes."

ESP

Dr. Dan flipped open the two tape recorders. He handed one of the tapes to me and put the other in a stack.

I returned to my seat on the couch.

Frankly, I was stunned. I'd been aware of my ability to "connect the dots" as I'd called it many times. It was how I got through life. What Dr. Barbara described dovetailed with my speculation that "vision," "discernment" or "comprehension" might be my Dharma. But I hadn't fully realized what this ability truly was, nor had I comprehended the extent to which this, this omni-perception, had been developed. It would take a while to absorb this information and to understand the implications.

One thing was apparent from my reading as well as from the other readings I'd just heard. Dharma is not a gift. It is a skill that has been developed over lifetimes.

Imagine spending almost an entire lifetime in a crow's nest.

I became too lost in thought to concentrate fully on the readings of others' Dharmas. After they were done, we were sent off in different directions to transcribe our tapes. After lunch we'd have a group discussion.

I went to the back porch where a table and chairs had

been set up. The clouds had just parted and the sun had come out. Yesterday's heat had been broken. The sky was a deep, rich blue, and it was pleasant, breezy and cool.

As I was writing out the reading in longhand and enjoying clean, dust-free air, I saw much that had gone past me when I'd been sitting in front of Dr. Barbara and listening. Here, for example, was a phrase I needed to ponder:

"The movement forward would be in the disseminating through interaction of the perception that this one does have."

Did that mean that I would benefit from teaching others how to develop omni-perception? Or did it mean that I would benefit from teaching others about my worldview? The words clearly stated that I should disseminate "the perception that this one does have." The accuracy of my perception of reality presumably benefited from my ability in the area of omniscient perception. The more I looked at that phrase, the more that interpretation seemed to be correct. Yet I had the feeling that a person could not understand or accept my worldview if they possessed no ability in the area of omni-perception. The two went hand in hand.

ESP

And "interaction." Obviously, that meant give and take. Dr. Barbara seemed to be saying it was the give and take that would allow me to understand better what I subconsciously already knew. Through interaction I could draw this out and make the most progress. At the same time, I'd help others advance.

I shook my head. At one time in my life I'd thought I wanted to be a teacher, but that was a long time ago. Being the head of an ad agency had resulted in burn out in the area of give and take. Also, a year prior I'd gone on the road and conducted a series of seminars to promote a book I'd written on how to follow a spiritual path to abundance. I hadn't particularly enjoyed conducting those seminars. For better or for worse, I might as well admit that I'd become an introspective guy who enjoyed the process of creation—creating ads, creating TV commercials, creating books—but did not particularly like getting out in front of people and interacting with them.

I sat back in my chair and gazed across the yard to a grove of trees and the edge of a forest beyond. I imagined what this part of Missouri must have been like when the first European settlers arrived. Perhaps it was not so different from today. The trees were large, so I doubted they were second growth.

ESP

There was still plenty of wildlife. I'd heard a sampling this morning during our group meditation and before bed last night when a coyote had howled. Probably, except for cleared areas, the land had not changed a great deal. Even so, a hundred and fifty years ago I'd be willing to bet even more wildlife had made this land home. The Indians would have done what they could to create conditions for wildlife to flourish, such as using controlled fires to clear areas so that grazing animals like deer would have places to feed. The Indians felt they were part of nature and held a special reverence for life. They wouldn't have over-hunted as the white man did.

I snapped out of my thoughts. Had I just been connecting the dots? Seeing the full picture where only part of it existed?

How did this omni-perception work?

I thought about the crow's nest and was reminded of someone I'd met a few months before. A California-based magazine had commissioned me to interview a University of Virginia professor, Jeffrey Hopkins, who was head of the Western world's largest Tibetan and Buddhist studies program. Dr. Hopkins, who'd just had a book published, had been on the staff of the Dalai Lama and had been an English interpreter for him when he traveled abroad.

ESP

I'd started by asking Dr. Hopkins what had gotten him interested in Eastern studies and Buddhism. He said he'd taken some time off between his junior and senior years in college and signed on with the crew of a freighter bound for Tahiti. The freighter had taken 45 days to get there.

I recalled that Dr. Hopkins had shifted in his chair. "Most of the time there was nothing to do, and so I began meditating on the sky. I really got into it. I ended up spending a year and a half away from college between my junior and senior years, plus half of a summer on a lake in Southern Quebec Province, and the other half on a river in Oklahoma. Frankly, I was getting a little too far out and needed help. One of my friends had heard about the Mongolian Tibetan Monks in New Jersey. So at the end of 1962 we paid them a visit."

Maybe spending a lifetime in a crow's nest was not so bizarre. Not if meditating on the sky was addictive as professor Hopkins seemed to indicate.

AFTER A HEARTY, HOMEGROWN, down on the farm lunch, we gathered in the living room. Laurel and Christine had each taken notes on each person's Dharma. We had each transcribed our readings and studied them. It was time for discussion.

People had a lot of questions. Most had to do with how an individual could put his or her Dharma to use in daily life.

Dr. Laurel said, "Your Dharma is the essence of who you are. It is part of you and you will almost certainly use it in whatever activity you choose. Of course, some activities will be better than others in terms of giving you an opportunity to serve humanity and feel fulfilled."

Dr. Laurel went on to say, "A good way to analyze any situation you may face is to divide it into three parts. First, what is the goal? In other words, what do you want to have happen? Obviously, in establishing a goal you need to clearly visualize the end result.

"Second, what is the purpose of the goal? In other words, why do you want it? Ultimately, the purpose of everything we do and experience on the physical plane is to become more like our Creator. So, when all is said and done, the purpose of the goal is the journey you take and the person you become in the process.

"Third, what activity is required? What can you spend your time doing that will create the journey that allows you to become more like your Creator and ultimately will lead you to your goal?" She paused and looked from one of us to the other. "So, look at your situation. If something doesn't seem to be working, chances are one of the three parts of the model is missing."

I was taking notes in my journal. I drew a line across the page and wrote:

My goal: Raise the level of awareness of mankind a notch.

Purpose: Know myself more deeply. Understand the big picture more thoroughly. Enjoy the act of creating. Become more like my Creator. Accomplish my mission/assignment.

Activity: Write books and teach the how of omni-perception and the true construct of reality.

Dr. Laurel said, "What I'd like you to do now is spend a few minutes thinking of how you've seen your Dharma manifest itself in your life. Then we'll go around the room and tell the others."

How had I seen my Dharma? Better yet, how hadn't I?

When my turn came I said, "I've been aware for a long time that I had a knack for seeing how things relate together in the big picture. What can and can't be. How if you change one thing, it can change everything. What is, and what probably isn't true. Of course, when I was young I didn't think this was unusual. As I got older it became apparent to me that not everyone had this ability. For example, I remember a Christmas when I was three or maybe four years old. On the morning of the big day my sister who was five years older than me said she'd heard Santa's reindeer on the roof the night before. I recall thinking, there's no way a guy in a sled pulled by reindeer could visit every house in the world in one night. One person couldn't do that no matter what kind of transportation he used. But I kept my mouth shut because I wasn't sure whether she was serious, or if she was telling this little story about the reindeer for my benefit. I kept up the pretense about Santa with all my classmates and everyone around me until they all finally caught on. That must have been when I was seven or eight. I didn't want to spoil their fun."

I looked at notes I'd made in my journal. "How has my Dharma, omni-perception, manifested in my life? Well, for starters it comes through in the type of novels I enjoy writing.

I've had some success with what at that time was a new

genre called 'visionary fiction,' a category recently established by the Library of Congress. The word 'visionary' is used in the sense that the author or the characters have an ability to see beyond the veil. Rather than being set only in physical reality as 99.99 percent of novels are, mine take into account the existence of a non-physical realm and the impact this realm has on people and events.

"To my way of thinking, a novel that doesn't factor in a person's soul purpose, or their karma from previous lives, or the fact that we are spiritual beings here on earth in physical bodies to learn, is only dealing with a small part of a much larger story. And something else. Life is a continuum. To have a story end at the end of a life may be to end the story in the middle. Or at the beginning. At least that's the way I see it, and when I tell a story I want to tell it all.

"Another way my ability for omni-perception manifests is kind of funny, really. In the case of many books and movies I'm able after about five minutes to see how the whole story is going to unfold. A point comes, often very early on, where everything just sort of clicks into place for me. What comes afterwards is so predictable that it's boring. There's no way the story can play out any differently unless the writer breaks all the rules. And writers who've made it to the level where they're writing for the movies or popular fiction don't break those kinds of rules. If I'm watching TV, for example, I'll switch to another channel or turn it off and go to bed."

I took a breath and looked around. Mainly I saw blank stares. "Up until today," I said, "I thought this ability to connect the dots, as I called it in the past, was a talent I was born with. Now I realize that it's a skill that's been developed."

After we finished going around the room and everyone had spoken, Dr. Laurel said, "What I'd like you to do now is draw a picture of your Dharma."

She passed around a book on something called Mind Mapping.

"You might want to use the technique explained in this book. You put the main idea in the middle, in this case your Dharma. And then the various ramifications that spread out from it."

I'd used Mind Mapping before to outline books. So I grabbed a large piece of paper and some crayons. First, I stopped by my room and found my wallet. I pulled out a dollar bill and studied the pyramid with the eye on top radiating light. Then I went to the dining room and sat down at the table. In the middle of the paper I drew a triangle with an eye inside. On the sides of the triangle I wrote "Body, mind, spirit." Then I drew rays of light shooting out from this to form a large circle, around which I wrote "all that is." Inside this circle I wrote "understanding what, why, how," and the words, "manifest" and "knowable." I divided the outside of the circle into a dark section and a light section. On one I wrote "yin." On the other, "yang." On one side starting in the dark section and continuing into the light, I wrote "unknowable." I did the same on the other side with the words "not manifest."

I studied my creation. Something wasn't quite right.

I went to the living room, found a pair of scissors on the coffee table and trimmed the corners until it was a circle.

It took the others a while longer to finish their mind maps, so show and tell came after dinner. When it got to me, I held up my drawing and said, "We're all part of the One Life. Each of us is a sliver of the energy and intelligence that in the western world calls God. We're like pieces of a hologram in the sense that each piece contains the whole picture. As such, every one of us is at the center of Creation looking out at our world, our reality, our creation—with both a small 'c' and a capital 'C.' The best way I know to get a sense of this is to stand on a mountain top. I have a home on a mountain in Virginia, and the summit is only a ten-minute walk. I go there to meditate whenever I can. Try it and you'll realize you are the center of everything."

I pointed to the middle of my drawing. "This triangle with an eye is me. Like you, I am both the creator and the creation. From my vantage point at the center I view my creation. I've labeled the sides of the triangle 'body, mind and spirit.' You see, anything physical such as a human body is like a triangle. Two sides must be in place before you have a third. The first two sides are spirit, which is life, and mind, which is the builder. The body is the result."

I took a breath and thought about Rupert Sheldrake, the English biochemist whose theory of morphogenetic fields fit perfectly with this explanation while it filled in the holes that currently exist in the theory of genetics and evolution. But this wasn't the time to get into that.

I continued by saying, "The circle of light around the triangle is all that is manifest, all that has come into being. This is

ESP

what can be known and what I seek to know. Outside the circle of light is all that is, as of now, not yet manifest, and therefore, is unknowable. I represent this with yin and yang that have not yet come together. They're only potential at this point."

I looked around. From the furrowed brows, I wasn't sure anyone understood a thing I'd said. No questions were asked.

After everyone had their turn at show and tell Laurel said, "I'd like you each to take a piece of paper and write down on it whatever might possibly keep you from expressing your Dharma, or whatever could keep you from accomplishing your life mission. These obstacles were mentioned in some of your reports. You might think of this potential blockage as a demon. You can draw a picture of it if you like."

Christine passed out sheets of paper. I took one and wrote, "Laziness."

After a couple of minutes later Laurel said, "In a minute we're going out on the front porch to have a ceremony. We are going to light a fire, and then we are going to burn those demons. I'll lead the ceremony but you are welcome to prepare a few words or a prayer to say before you burn your demon."

Night had come, and the rain had returned. It was cool and damp outside. The sounds of insects closed in on me. Beyond the porch was inky black forest.

A large metal trash can had been placed at the far end of the porch. Dr. Dan balled up some paper, lit it, and threw it in. Laurel said a prayer beseeching God to help us accomplish our missions, overcome our demons and practice our Dharmas. One after the other each of us went to the can and tossed in our paper. When my turn came, I stopped before the blaze and said, "Lord of the universe, Higher Self, I know that only laziness can keep me from a full understanding of You and of my Dharma, omni-perception. Therefore, having no need for laziness, I offer this demon to you in flame. I burn it, and in so doing convert it into energy that I convey to you as an offering."

That night when I went to bed, I told my Higher Self that I wanted to know just how this omni-perception works so that I could explain it to others.

I WOKE UP EARLY ON SUNDAY MORNING. It was a good morning to stay in bed and think. Rain was still gently falling, and I felt cozy and warm under the covers. A lot had gone on the day before and there was much to think about. The question that really had me stumped was, how could I teach others about how omni-perception works when I didn't know myself? I'd thought it was a gift. I hadn't tried to analyze how it worked.

The UVa professor popped into my mind, the man I'd interviewed for the California-based magazine. As I lay in bed in Windyville, Missouri listening to the rain gently falling, I recalled how I'd misjudged how long it would take to drive from my office in Richmond to Charlottesville that day. His office was in one of the buildings that lines the "Lawn" at the University.

I'd parked my car across the street, and made a beeline in the direction of the Rotunda, a historic building designed by and built under the supervision of Thomas Jefferson. I hurried past students who strolled red brick walkways and sat on steps reading or talking. I stopped one to ask directions, and found my way a down flight of steps and into the office of Jeffrey Hopkins.

We exchanged pleasantries. I pulled a tape recorder from my briefcase. "I hope you don't mind if I use this," I said. "Keeps me from having to take notes."

"No problem."

"I understand that the Dalai Lama is coming to Northern California," I said.

"Yes, he's coming to the West Coast and briefly to the East Coast, to Washington."

"What's his mission?" I asked.

Professor Hopkins said, "I assume it is to spread his message of compassion, of not accepting the way things appear, and the need to develop the wisdom to penetrate appearances."

Penetrate appearances. Now I knew why that interview came to mind.

I asked the professor if he would tell me about the Dalai Lama. Among other things he said, "I'd say that he worked very hard to develop a message that would be suitable not just for Buddhists, not just for religious people, but for the whole world."

"Can you distill that message?"

"It is to recognize that everyone wants happiness, and doesn't want suffering. That everybody is like oneself in that very important respect, and that we need to act from within that recognition. It's very easy for us each just to say, 'Oh right,' and then go on being selfish. But to recognize that and to see that other people have a right to get rid of suffering, and that we shouldn't use them to try to gain our happiness, and to make the kindness that results from this realization the very basis for society. The Dalai Lama once said, and it's in my book, that 'society is kindness.' I thought, well, that's his broken English. But now I realize it wasn't broken English. In fact, what he said has a real wallop to it."

I said, "So the idea is that someone you might consider your enemy, or totally unscrupulous, is striving for the same thing you want through their own methods?"

Professor Hopkins said, "Yes, and we cannot fail to notice that some people's methods for gaining happiness and getting rid of suffering are really weird and wrong. We need to help them learn how to stop those methods. But nevertheless, their goal is happiness, just as ours is."

I felt my brow furrow. "Isn't that the purpose of karma? To teach us what works and what doesn't?"

Hopkins said, "I don't know if it's the purpose of karma. Karma just is. So often we suffer and don't learn a thing."

"But if the boomerang keeps coming back at us, when what goes around eventually comes around, after a few times shouldn't we say, 'What a minute, how come this keeps coming back at me?'

Hopkins said, "Thus is the purpose of teaching—to alert one to what's possibly going on. To encourage people to reflect."

I asked the professor about his new book.

He smiled. "The principle is the one the Dalai Lama keeps repeating, which is, 'Just as I want to alleviate my suffering, so does this person.' It tells how to cultivate this attitude in meditation by reflecting on individual persons one after another, starting with friends and working to less strong friends, then working to people whom you know but haven't paid much attention to. Then you progress to difficult people, then to the least of your enemies, and one by one proceed hopefully to some of your worst enemies."

I popped out of my reverie and back to Missouri. Seeing things from another's point of view. Meditating so that you get inside another's skin. Pretty basic, I thought. But nevertheless it could be a key. Maybe for a lot of people it's not something they do very often—not something they have even thought about.

I decided to think about that at a later time. For the moment I wanted to return to that conversation in Virginia. I could still picture the professor. He had the most pleasant smile.

I said to the professor, "Isn't that what Jesus said? To pray for your enemies?"

"Yes, and to hate the sin not the sinner. Don't make the person the object of your problem. Make the attitude the problem. Christianity is well known for its care and compassion for others," he said.

"Jesus also said that God makes his rain to fall and his sun to shine on the wicked and the good."

Hopkins nodded. "Yes, and there is also a lot of emphasis on helping the poor and the downtrodden."

"If someone reads your book, *Cultivating Compassion,* and they strive to do just that, what is the end goal to be achieved?"

Hopkins gave a little shrug. "The goal in this system is to get to an increasingly more developed level where one can help others more and more. It's not to disappear in Nirvana or anything like that."

"So helping others through service is the path?"

Hopkins said, "It is both the path and the goal. The perfection of mind and body is for the sake of enabling one to provide service.

"What else do you want people to know about your book?"

"It lays out the steps for developing compassion and provides techniques for getting around problems that arise in trying to do this. The exercises given are very clear."

I asked, "Would you classify your book as a workbook?"

"It certainly is a workbook. The meditative exercises are in bold type and in between are descriptions of how to do it. It's designed to help lead the person towards the development of compassion. At minimum, one gets an idea of what some other people are doing. At maximum, one does it oneself and improves a little. What more can one ask?"

My mind drifted back to the present. Being able to put oneself in another's shoes was only part of what was necessary in developing omni-perception. But the reality behind what the professor had said opened a door in my mind.

I pulled back the covers and got out of bed. Thoughts swirled. I reached for a pen and my journal and began to write furiously. When I got back to Richmond, I'd start a new book. This weekend would be part of it.

Chapter Three

Develop the Right Mindset

After meditating on the matter and giving it considerable thought, I'm convinced that everyone has the capacity for omni-perception, which to my mind is simply ESP, or intuition on steroids. All minds are connected. They form one Universal Mind, which in other books I refer to as "Infinite Mind." This means that everything there is to see or know is inside you. You simply need to develop your ability to access it.

We each have a conscious mind, an unconscious mind and a subconscious mind that is ours alone. But at a deep level our subconscious minds merge. Moreover, at the very core of our being is the Infinite Mind, the mind of God, or Cosmic Mind. Therefore, your mind and my mind contain all knowledge, truth, and wisdom, past, present and future.

In exploring how to draw out information you wish to attain, it will help to have a working theory of the mind. The one that makes sense to me is that promulgated by the School of Metaphysics. According to this theory, three divisions of mind exist. The first is the Super Conscious Mind, the second is the Subconscious, and the third is the Conscious Mind.

Seven divisions are present within the three levels of consciousness. The First Level is Cosmic Consciousness. It's the part of you that's God. It is also called the Buddha or Christ Consciousness.

The Second Level is where your subconscious mind joins the Super Conscious or Cosmic Consciousness. It is also where your subconscious mind meets the subconscious minds of others, where those of like mind or compatible goals and desires are rounded up to become part of your life. You help them, and they help you realize your goals and desires.

The Third level is that part of your subconscious mind where things begin for you as a separate individual. It is where desire takes root and begins to form reality. For example, you see a shiny new Porsche automobile and you think to yourself, "I really want a car like that." If this is a true desire, a seed has been planted that will grow until the desire is fulfilled.

The Fourth Level is where the physical begins. Here vibrations become separate. This is the beginning of you as an individual and it continues into the Fifth Level where vibrations divide into hot or cold, black or white, male or female. Between the Fourth and Fifth Levels are the Akashic Records, what you might think of as in internet terms as the "cloud storage" area, or universal memory bank of humankind, containing all the thoughts and actions of people and associated events that have ever taken place since human life began on Earth.

The Sixth Level is the emotional level—where our emotions originate. It is the place from which feelings come that we experience in our bodies, and as such, it is the level that is most closely related to the physical. Whenever you *feel* strongly about something, your subconscious mind is pushing that something out into the open for you to consider, and perhaps, to deal with.

The Seventh Level, which is the conscious mind, has two parts—the unconscious part of the conscious mind and the conscious part of the conscious mind.

We're all familiar with the conscious mind, the place where our attention remains most of the time when we're awake. It's what registers impulses from the sense organs (ears, eyes, nerves, taste buds, and so forth) that travel to the brain and are translated into the sensations of sight, sound, hearing, touch, taste and smell.

The conscious part of the conscious mind is the part where you are aware of what's happening. You touch, taste or see something. Impulses travel along nerves such as the optic nerve from the eye to the brain, where an event takes place. Let's say you take a bite of a chocolate bar. You immediately recognize the flavor. That's the Conscious Mind at work. To identify the flavor, your Conscious Mind calls upon the memory of the taste of chocolate stored in its unconscious part.

What other functions does the unconscious part of the Conscious mind perform? Let's say you get into your car to go somewhere. You turn the key, you release the brake, you drive. You don't have to think much about what you're doing. If you're like me, you may drive along thinking about something else and take a turn that you normally take even though today you were going somewhere else and shouldn't take that turn. After a few blocks you realize you're on the wrong road. The unconscious, programmed part of you led you astray.

The unconscious part of your Conscious Mind is in fact programmed very much like a computer. Remember the first time you got behind the wheel? That time when you turned the key and released the brake you had to pay close attention to every detail in order to make the automobile operate smoothly. You had to watch all the buttons, people, stoplights and so on. Over the months and years that you've been driving, however, your Conscious Mind made all those details a part of you. They slipped into the unconscious part of your Conscious Mind as surely as a computer program is loaded onto a hard drive.

All the pieces of information you've come in contact with in this life are stored in the unconscious part of your Conscious Mind, including information that in a practical sense you've forgotten or never fully understood. Erroneous information is there. For example, as a child perhaps your parents said, "Don't go out in the dark by yourself, or the boogie man will get you." They didn't explain about the boogieman. So, within the unconscious part of your Conscious Mind today is information that says if you go out into the dark something bad is surely going to get you. You didn't question the information when it was programmed in because it came from someone in authority. But it's still there, and it's keeping you from going out at night.

You don't have to be doomed, however, to stay at home at night for the rest of your life. Bringing that information out of the unconscious mind, looking at it rationally and subjecting it to analysis with the conscious part of the Conscious Mind will release the fear. The problem for most of us is that it's just too scary or too painful, or maybe we're just too lazy to examine our unconscious programming. This is the major block that negates a person's ability for omni-perception.

Let me give you an example. For many years the body of the Great Sphinx at Giza, Egypt, was covered with sand because it is lower than the surrounding area. Originally, the part of the Sphinx that is now the head was an outcropping of rock on a plain. The rest of the rock was uncovered and carved into the body. Over the years sand storms had covered it up again. But today the sand has been cleared away and the body is clearly visible. A geologist happened to notice not long ago that the body of the Sphinx appeared to have been worn by water erosion. Small gullies had formed all over it. Other geologists were consulted. The type of rock that the Sphinx is made of was compared with the same type of rock that indeed had been worn away by water. Sure enough, the Sphinx's body had suffered water erosion.

The problem, of course, is that the Sphinx is smack in the middle of a desert where it almost never rains. According to textbooks, Egyptologists, and tradition, the head of the Sphinx is a portrait of King Khafre of Egypt who lived about 4500 years ago, and that's when the Sphinx is supposed to have been created. Yet meteorologists who study weather patterns say the climate of Giza, Egypt, was pretty much the same 4500 years ago as it is today. For there to have been enough rain to cause the type of erosion in evidence, the Sphinx would have to have been in existence for more than twice that. Way back then the weather of the area would have been similar to the African savanna with a season when rain poured down for several months.

Now when I heard this, my initial reaction was that the Sphinx must be a heckuva lot older than anyone previously thought. A civilization must have created it that predated the Egyptians. Indeed, such a theory has been put forth. Close examination of the Sphinx itself reveals that the original head may have been reworked into its present form that resembles King Khafre. It doesn't take a great deal of thought or imagination to picture an ancient civilization of hunter-gatherers on the savanna digging out the outcropping that is now the Sphinx and carving it into the shape of a giant animal—in all probability, a lion. What we know about ancient Homo sapiens indicates that humans had the mental capacity to have accomplished such a task as long ago as 40,000 years—or perhaps many, many more. Consider for instance the cave paintings in France that date back that far. It isn't difficult to imagine the Egyptians coming along later and adapting an already ancient monolith to their own purposes.

What do you suppose, however, that the scientific community of Egyptologists thinks of all this?

Their reaction has been to reject it out of hand.

Why do you suppose?

Several possibilities spring to mind. First, these Egyptologists have a whole host of notions and information, much of which may be erroneous, stored in their unconscious minds that may cause a knee-jerk rejection of the idea that the Sphinx could possibly be more than 4500 years old. To accept the idea they'd have to give up their belief that Ancient Egypt was home to the first civilized people. For many this may be a matter of pride. Second, they might have to rethink their religious faith. Many Egyptologists are located in Egypt or the Middle East and they are followers of Islam. Islam traces its founding to Ishmael, a son of Abraham, the patriarch of the Jews. So, like Christians and Jews, followers of Islam trace their roots to Abraham and from him to Adam and Eve and the Garden of Eden. Calculations based on the listing in the Old Testament of forebears of Abraham back to Adam indicate that the human race could not be more than 4500 to 5000 years old. It could be, then, that religious beliefs programmed into the unconscious minds of Egyptologists prevent them from accepting the truth just as similar programming prevents many Christian fundamentalists from accepting evolution. This programming may literally create a mental block.

Conscious Minds, including both the unconscious and the conscious parts, contain the data, information and beliefs with which individuals define themselves. Often, this is referred to as the ego. If a person's definition includes "Biblical inerrantist" in it, all kinds of things must rejected out of hand in order to maintain this part of the identity. The person cannot accept that anything is more than 5,000 years old. He must hold that all plants and animals came into being in their present forms, and so forth. To accept anything as true that does not go along with Biblical literalism is to relinquish the person's identity.

The same is true for Scientific Materialists who continue to maintain that nothing exists except material substance in spite of a huge amount of evidence to the contrary. Many even dispute that the Big Bang took place even—though there is overwhelming evidence that it did—because, if the universe had a beginning, simple logic indicates something, or someone, must have created it.

How can people that are in denial and therefore stuck with an outdated worldview bring their thinking up to date and begin to develop their latent powers of omni-perception? It isn't easy, but with a conscious effort it can be done. Here's how I look at it. I think of a person's identity or ego—mine included—as a big stack of cans of peas at the grocery store that forms a pyramid. Each can represents an individual belief. Remove or attempt to change one at the bottom of the stack, and the whole thing is likely to come tumbling down.

Then the pyramid has to be rebuilt from the ground up in a way that works and fits together neatly. Rather than go through the pain and effort that would be required, the easiest course is to reject information that would force one to remove or change the position of a can. That's precisely what most people do. They reject the new information. It's an automatic reaction that's done without any thought. It's also what blocks them from exercising the ability of omni-perception.

When I look back at my life I realize that my worldview has been revised dozens if not hundreds of times. Maybe thousands. It is perhaps more accurate to say that it has been and continues to be in a state of constant evolution. Each time a new piece of information comes to light that forces me to replace a can of peas, I've replaced that can whether or not it required me to rebuild the entire pyramid from the ground up. One cannot see the whole if one rejects a part.

In addition to being difficult and requiring effort, this practice of accepting truth and revising our mental model of reality can be painful. It can be painful on the level of a worldview and it can be painful on a personal world level as well. Let's say, for example, that you are presented with a fact that requires you to accept that your wife or husband is cheating on you. You can ignore the fact or you can accept it and change your personal world model accordingly. Obviously, this may be very hard to do. The same is true for someone who clings to his or her identity as a Biblical inerrantist, or to Scientific Materialist—or to the idea that Egypt is the first and oldest civilization on earth.

At some level, however, you know the truth whether or not you deny it. It's in your subconscious mind. It's also in the minds of others and you are connected to them. And it's in the Super Conscious Mind. You will have to build a dike around the unpleasant fact in order to keep it out of your conscious mind, and keeping it blocked off in this manner will cause it to fester. The truth will be presented to you in dreams, which you may also choose to ignore. It may manifest as an anxiety attack. It may surface in the form of an illness. Your subconscious mind or Higher Self wants you to know the truth. These sorts of things are what your subconscious mind or Higher Self uses to get your attention. Knowing and facing the truth is the way for you to grow. Growth and evolution are why you are on earth in physical form. Once you stop evolving, your days on earth are numbered. It follows, then, that nothing is more important than pursuing the truth and bringing it into the conscious part of your Conscious Mind. Nothing is more important than doing what you can to further your personal evolution. Your mental and physical health depends on it. The upshot of all this is that doing your best to develop your ability for omni-perception is the right course of action no matter how painful it may be.

For me, omni-perception has become like driving a car or riding a bicycle. It works for me without any conscious thought. In fact how it's done is no longer only in my unconscious mind. I've been working at it so long and over so many lifetimes that it's become part of my Subconscious Mind or Soul. The result is that I have to stop to think about how it is done in order to explain the process to someone else. And like riding a bike, how it's done is not always obvious. When you ride a bike and start to fall, for instance, you lean in the direction of the fall and turn the wheel to guide yourself back into an upright position. You don't lean away from the direction you feel you might fall, which is what logic would indicate.

Over the time I've been analyzing how omni-perception is done, I've observed that some people have a tendency to come to it easily, and that others have a rough time of it. This tendency, or lack thereof, appears to be part of an individual's personality or makeup. As a result, I can get an indication of whether or not people possess the tendency by talking to them. For example, I might ask if they were forced to choose between "practical," or "innovative," which adjective would they select to describe themselves? Those who see themselves as innovators are likely to be better bets in developing their innate ability for omni-perception.

An individual who will have a difficult time is one who will describe himself as firmly grounded in reality. He or she will say he wants facts. He or she remembers facts. This seems reasonable enough until one stops and thinks about what is really going on. These facts may be small parts of the big picture, but by focusing on them almost exclusively, the person may miss the forest for the trees. On the other hand, the individual who has potential to grasp the big picture is likely to focus on the future and the possibilities it holds. The "possible" is always in front of them, pulling on the imagination like a magnet. The future holds an attraction that details, minutiae and tradition do not.

A difference can also be seen in the way two people process information. The one who will have difficulty achieving omni-perception will be the one who can never have enough data. True to their preference for details over vision, they want facts. Lots of them. Once they have collected a pile, they will want more. It may seem that they can never have enough before they will even consider changing their mind about anything. They simply don't want to go through the pain and bother of having to rearrange that pyramid of cans.

On the other hand, the omniscient individual does not continue gathering information *ad nauseam*. She wants and values data to be sure. But once she has enough to see a pattern, or to support a hunch or theory, she will begin rearranging the pyramid based on the pattern or coherence that he sees. For her, the information simply "hangs together" in a way that means the old pyramid must be scrapped. The old one no longer supports the facts. The omniscient individual may continue gathering data after she is already convinced in her own mind, but this will be done more to prove a point to potential naysayers than for her own edification.

Although the omniscient one is tolerant of the way things are and how things usually are done, he will abandon any procedures or dogma that can be shown to be counterproductive or indifferent to the goals they seemingly serve. Not so with those who are stuck in the past. They are so in tune with established, time-honored institutions and ways of doing things that they simply cannot understand those who wish to abandon or change long-held beliefs and ideas of how reality operates. If it was good enough for granddaddy, it should be good enough for the current generation.

I've met and worked with many who fall into one category or the other just described. Under normal circumstances, individuals who fall on the side of tradition and the past can be wonderful and warm individuals. It is possible to be narrow minded and nice. It simply isn't part of their makeup to be visionaries. To develop omni-perception requires someone who is constantly on the lookout for new and better ways of explaining things, someone who is stimulated by possibilities, and is constantly motivated by a restless feeling that the truth is out there if we will only take the effort to go and find it.

My experience with stick-in-the-muds and with those who have potential for omni-perception comes primarily from my many years as a business executive. Depending on the organization, individuals with what it takes to be omniscient may not stand out from the crowd. In younger days he may have raised his head out of the foxhole and been shot at enough times that he learned to keep a low profile. The end result is, the person may be cautious about revealing his tendency toward open-mindedness. After a while, like most people, he may have become stuck in the trap of conventionality. It may take some coaxing to get him to venture out of his shell to take a new look at how the world actually works.

Once I was involved with a company that was trying to institute new procedures that gave more authority and autonomy to people at lower levels in the organization. The new approach also eliminated a couple of layers of management.

Nevertheless, great improvements in operations had been experienced wherever the system had been successfully implemented. Several times I sat through a presentation that was designed to demonstrate that this way of working resulted in increased productivity, higher quality work and greater attentiveness on the part of workers. The upshot was that customers were extremely satisfied and repeat sales strong. Two upper level managers also sat through the presentation with me. I'd say we each saw it three times. At first neither of these managers held much enthusiasm for the changes that would be required to implement the new approach.

Nevertheless, one of those managers became one of the biggest agents of change in the company, even though originally he had not accepted the concept.

The other manager turned out to be a dedicated obstructionist even though he also saw the presentation three times and the presentation offered some very compelling facts and examples to support the case for change. It simply was not part of this manager's makeup to embrace something new that would mean abandoning time-honored ways of doing things, even under pressure from his superiors. He was too wedded to tradition. He preferred "proven" ways of operating and chose the likelihood of having to find another job rather than implement change he could not bring himself to embrace.

We might infer from this that when presented with a concept that isn't part of their belief system, even potential omniscient folks may appear to dismiss it without much thought. This was indeed the case with the manager who eventually did come around. If he'd seen the presentation only once, I doubt that he would have embraced the new concept. The upshot is, an effort may be needed to get some people to open their minds. Repetition may be required. Sitting through a presentation of new concepts several times, for example, might make a difference.

As the principal of an advertising agency, I spent years and hundreds of thousands of dollars studying the effects of various amounts of exposure to advertising. What I learned was this. The first time a person sees something new, whether it's an ad or anything else, their reaction usually is to categorize what is seen in terms of existing knowledge. Suppose, for example, a person sees a purple cow. The reaction might be summed up as, "What is that? Oh, it's a cow, isn't it? Yes. Except, it's a purple cow." Once they've got this in a pigeonhole, they feel free to move on.

The second time they see the cow, their reaction is likely to be more personally evaluative. "Ah-ha. There's that purple cow again. Odd. But what does it mean to me?"

If they feel a purple cow holds relevance for them, the third and subsequent exposures will reinforce this feeling. They may take action after the second exposure, or many more may be required to push them over the line. Our change agent, for example, got on board after only three exposures to the presentation.

If a person decides that a purple cow has no relevance, or that it doesn't go along with their established belief system, a person may well think there must be some mistake. He or she may unconsciously believe that by ignoring the facts, they will go away. "This isn't happening," he or she may say. "If I just nod my head and smile, this will blow over." This is one form of denial.

But let's say the person presenting the new data sticks to their guns. Next will be anger. Our Egyptologists might say, "You can't be serious. Look at what all the textbooks say. No one has ever found any evidence that there was a civilization that predates Egypt. You can't force me to believe this."

Let's imagine that the person presenting the facts pulls out even more and sticks to his guns. Bargaining follows.

"Okay, I understand now. It does look a little bit like water erosion. But I'm sure that doesn't mean the Sphinx wasn't built by the Egyptians. Who knows what the climate of Giza was like 4500 years ago? Just change your theory a little and I'm sure we'll be able to accept it."

Once more, the water erosion theorists hold their ground. The fourth stage is depression. A change may be evident in a person's body language. Slumped shoulders. Dark circles under the eyes. It's as though the individual were saying, "I've tried to tell them, and they won't listen. There's no way someone besides the Egyptians built the Sphinx. It's in every textbook in every library in the world. But they just won't listen."

Once he or she has reached this stage, the new theory has practically been accepted. All that is required for them to come around is more time and reinforcement of the message. If you are the one pushing the new theory, it's time now to give your Egyptology colleagues some slack. Tell them, "Chin up, and let's get on with it. The Egyptians created a magnificent civilization. Nothing can change that." Then, it's only a matter of time before the fifth and last stage is reached, which is acceptance. Now you've got yourself a convert.

The conclusion I've come to is that repetition can be important and helpful in changing people's minds, but only if those potential converts have potential for developing omniperception. They must be open-minded by nature and possess a built-in uneasiness about holding onto ideas that aren't fully supported by the facts. My experience suggests, however, that those qualities are rare, and so it's probably naive to think that a very large percentage of people who have been thinking a certain way all their lives are going to embrace a new paradigm without a significant period of adjustment. To do so, they will have to give up ideas and concepts they are accustomed to, a way of thinking they've grown fond of and are comfortable with, one that's worked for them just fine and brought them where they are today. It's like saying goodbye to an old friend. It may even be as traumatic as getting divorced.

Suffice it to say, it isn't easy to set aside the ideas and assumptions of a lifetime and accept a whole new paradigm. To do so on a routine basis, as I have conditioned myself to do, requires not so much setting aside the ego or conscious mind, it requires a sense of self that isn't based on traditional, transient definitions. No matter how you may define yourself today, let me assure you that you are much, much more than

ESP

a Southern Baptist, or a housewife, a computer programmer, or college president. You are a child of the universe. You are a spark of energy and intelligence from the light that is God. You're a piece of the hologram. "All that Is" is contained in you. You have evolved to a very high form already, and you will continue to evolve to a much higher form whether or not you accept what I have said to you today.

As a child of God, it is important to be open minded about new information comes your way. Once you accept this new definition of yourself as a spark from the Divine Light, new information requiring rearrangement of worldview cannot and will not change who you are. Nothing can harm you.

Perhaps you say, "Why bother? I'm happy thinking of myself the way I have for the last twenty, thirty, fifty or more years."

The most important reason is that knee jerk reactions based on old definitions aren't going to help you grow. And you've got to keep growing or your Higher Self is going to decide that you've learned all you're going to learn in this incarnation so it's time for you to return home and be recycled. This happened to my sister. She led an active life. She raised four children. She had a productive career. She was offered early retirement and she took it. She sat around the house for a year and watched soap operas. She slept late. She didn't do anything to stimulate her mind. And approximately 18 months after she accepted that golden handshake, she died from a malignant brain tumor—at the age of 61.

The doctors could not explain why she came down with the tumor. "Just one of those things that happens sometimes." Not hereditary. Not something you catch at the shopping mall. Simply bad luck.

The doctors didn't know why, but I did. She needed a way to exit the earth plane because she had stopped growing. Her personal evolution in this lifetime had become arrested. There was no reason to remain here. There's no reason for anyone to stay on earth when that happens—unless the person is contributing to someone else's growth. That wasn't the case with my sister. What happened was predictable. Her Higher Self called her home.

The bottom line is this. Set aside your pride. It's based on the old, temporal you, anyway. Set aside your fears. Nothing can harm you. You are immortal. Develop a willingness—no, an eagerness to update your worldview—as many times as it takes. Grow into your full potential. As the old TV commercial for the U. S. Army says, "Be all that you can be."

Chapter Four
Entrain Your Mind

In his book, *The Seven Habits of Highly Effective People,* Stephen Covey writes about a realization that altered his life. He was wandering among stacks of books in a college library when he came across one that drew his interest. He opened it and was so moved by what he read that he reread the paragraph many times. It contained the simple idea that a gap exists between stimulus and response, and that the key to our growth and happiness is how we use this gap. We have the power of choice in that fraction of a second. If we see a photograph of a creamy banana split, we can choose to order and eat it, or we can decide on raspberry sherbet—or no dessert at all. If we are presented with information that indicates the Sphinx is much older than we thought, we can choose to dismiss it out of hand. Or we can take a more careful look. We may find in the process that the legacy of humankind goes back much farther than we thought.

Richard Carlson, the author of *Don't Sweat the Small Stuff ... and It's All Small Stuff,* picks up on the same idea. His advice is always to take a breath before speaking or taking action. If you adopt this approach, you'll rid yourself of the habit of reacting. You'll begin taking a considered approach, and taking a considered approach can lead to all sorts of good things such as better relationships with friends, family, and co-workers. It can lead to a slimmer waist. It can even lead to your transformation from a five-sensory human being to one whose intuition and innate ability for omni-perception is highly developed.

Another way to grow, evolve and learn the art of omni-perception is to become what some have called a "silent observer" of yourself. The idea is to move your point of view out of your head, and place it on your shoulder or the ceiling. Then watch yourself go about your business. Once you start keeping an eye out, you may start to see things that aren't helping you get where you want to go. From this realization, it's a short step to self-transformation. Especially if you take that breath before reacting.

What else can you do?

The answer is, "Whatever helps you to entrain your mind."

What is meant by entraining the mind? According to my

dictionary the word entrain means "to pull or draw along after itself; to go aboard a train; or to put aboard a train." But the way I mean this word is different. Remember those levels of mind I wrote about in Chapter Three? There were seven of them. Contained within these levels of mind is everything known to man or woman—past, present, and possibly future. So all the truth you'll ever need in order to grow and evolve into the highest form there is can be found within your own mind. The trick is locating it and getting it to the conscious part of your Conscious Mind. That's where entrainment enters in. You need to get those levels of mind all lined up like the cars of a train so the information you need flows from one to the other until it reaches the surface.

I use several techniques to do this. Meditation is one.

Some people use meditation for relaxation. I use it to get at Truth. Perhaps this is why for me, repeating a mantra doesn't do much. The Truth can't flow to me if I'm constantly uttering the word "Ooomm," or "One," or "Blueberry."

I have a couple of ways of meditating. One is to sit quietly, back straight, feet on the floor, and relax. I'll ask my Higher Self or God a question to which I've been seeking an answer. Then I simply wait patiently and enjoy the silence.

ESP

Whenever what I identify as a monkey-mind thought enters my mind, I simply push it away. An example of a monkey mind thought is, "Did I remember to turn off the oven?" Or "I wonder what's for lunch today?" Or "Man, oh man, that report is due tomorrow. I'd better stop this and get oh it."

Eventually an idea or thought will come to me that is germane. If not, after ten minutes or so, I'll go on to something else confident that eventually what I need to know will be revealed.

Perhaps the most common way for me to entrain my mind, however, is to take a long walk, usually for about forty-five minutes. I do this three or four times a week. Sometimes there will be a question I'm wrestling with, and at other times there won't be anything specific on my mind.

There's something about being out in nature that opens the channel to the inner levels of my mind. I start by taking in the trees and shrubs and flora, and it usually occurs to me that this flora and fauna, including squirrels, birds, chipmunks and so forth are the outward representation of the spiritual dimension that supports and informs reality. I recognize that I am part of this. I realize that the Conscious Mind part of me that's thinking this is the tip of an iceberg poking out of an ocean of mind and that in this ocean of mind are the answers to all my questions. After a bit I become lost in reverie. Ideas start to flow. They may be ideas about how to solve a problem at work. Or something I can do to help another person. Or a stock I should invest in. If I'm working on a book or novel, ideas for it will come gushing through. When I get home from such a walk I usually rush to pick up a pad and pen in order to write all the ideas down. I've found that if I don't, they quickly fade away. I also keep a pad and pencil by my bedside in case ideas come to me in dreams.

Focusing on a particular place or thing is another effective way I've found to entrain my mind. On that weekend in Missouri I started getting information about the Indians and what the land was like before the first European settlers arrived. This happens wherever I go, and I believe it is normal. Evidence exists that places and things—from human cells to rocks—contain memories. I think of these memories as being located in the space between subatomic particles. A book that outlines a theory that suggests a scientific basis for this is *The Living Energy Universe,* by Gary E. R. Schwartz and Linda G. S. Russek.

ESP

In the jargon of metaphysics, tapping into memory of this kind is called psychometry, which is the ability to perceive information about people or events associated with an object by touching or being near it.

In July 2001, when I was at the School of Metaphysics for a weekend on developing intuition we performed a number of exercises to test, stretch and exercise our powers of intuition. For one of these experiments, we each brought from home an object that had meaning for us. On Saturday morning we put our objects in a pile in such a way that the others couldn't see which object belonged to which attendee. Then each of us selected an object from the pile. We were asked to meditate on it and then report to the others what came to mind.

I picked up what looked like a wedding ring. At first I thought of white dresses and black limousines and a big cake with bride and groom dolls on top. This was monkey-mind stuff simply associated with weddings in general and somehow I knew it. I concentrated on the ring and closed my eyes. What came to me then was a picture of a beach of white sand, bright blue water and burning blue sky with small, white, puffy clouds. I noticed the water was rough and there were lots of whitecaps. I'd vacationed on the Mediterranean and had the misfortune of experiencing a mistral, or windstorm, so I knew that a clear sky and white caps indicated high wind.

When my turn came for show and tell, I held it up for the others to see. "This looks like it's probably a wedding ring. At first I got a lot of stuff about weddings, such as cakes and white dresses, but that's probably just my mind associating with weddings in general. After a minute or two, I got an image that doesn't necessarily relate to weddings." And I explained about the image of the beach and the water and the whitecaps.

When I'd finished, the lady to whom the ring belonged raised her hand. She said, "It is a wedding ring, my mother's. But it wasn't given to her by my father at their wedding. You see, she lost her original ring. My father gave her this one to replace it. He waited until they were together on the beach in Barbados. They were on the windward side of the island where, guess what—there's almost always a high wind and the sea is usually quite rough."

A number of phenomena that fall into the categories of ESP or intuition exist without question. Yet the scientific establishment still does not recognize them. Egos cause denial among otherwise intelligent individuals and they cause experiments to fail that otherwise would prove the existence of these phenomena. The truth is, attitudes and beliefs of the researchers make a critical difference in the scientific investigation of ESP. As in all matters of the mind, belief is paramount. Double blind clinical tests have proven that those who do not believe ESP are unable to duplicate experiments that have been carried out successfully by researchers who do believe. I recently saw a segment on the Discovery TV channel that demonstrated this. Two researchers conducted the same experiment in the same laboratory using the same equipment. One researcher believed ESP was valid and the other did not. Both tests were supervised by impartial observers, including the Discovery Channel TV crew

The experiment was constructed as follows. A subject was seated in a sealed room with a TV camera trained on them. The researcher sat in another room with a TV monitor and a computer that would randomly select a time when a shield was to be lifted or dropped in front of the TV monitor. The researcher was to stare at the person on the screen of the TV monitor when the shield was up. The person in the other room with a TV camera trained on them was to record when she felt she was being watched. This individual was also wired

ESP

with an EKG to measure physiological changes that might occur when she was being watched or not being watched.

The experiment that employed the researcher who believed in ESP had a statistically significant number of correct scores, indicating that the experiment was a success. In other words, the percentage of correct "hits" could not have occurred by chance. On the other hand, the percentage of correct hits for the experiment that employed the doubting Thomas researcher fell within parameters that could be accounted for by chance. So this experiment failed to prove the validity of ESP. Nevertheless, the point of both experiments was made. ESP works for those who believe it does. It does not work for those who don't. Non believing researchers cannot validate ESP because they do not believe in it. This demonstrates the metaphysical law that people receive the outcome they expect. As metaphysicians have known for millennia, the power of belief is strong.

Unfortunately, most of us have been conditioned since birth to discount what is often described as intuition. As a result, we've developed a habit of not listening to what comes from the inner levels of mind. If we are to reconnect, the first step is to acknowledge that intuition is real, and that it is possible to be in touch. This "being in touch" is characterized by a sense of knowing, but not in the ordinary way that requires a subject (you) and an object (what is known). For example, you know that Virginia is on the east coast of North America. That's subject and object knowing. It exists outside of you. With the intuitive knowledge of the inner levels of mind, no separation exists between knower and known. An example might be your "knowledge" of how to ride a bicycle or ski, or my knowledge of how omni-perception operates. Until I have carefully observed and have thought of the correct words to use, it is difficult to explain what I know. I just know. Riding a bike, skiing, and omni-perception are each part of my being. Like intuition.

The three examples above pertain to knowledge that exists in your subconscious mind. Through meditation and other means we can also venture into the subconscious minds of others and even the Cosmic Mind. The route to these lies within us. We are the All, which includes Virginia and North America, and so we know where they stand with respect to one another.

To get my mind around this, it helps me to visualize the whole of humankind as a huge assembly of icebergs floating on an ocean covering a globe. The tip of each iceberg represents a

Conscious Mind. Below the water line, individual Subconscious Minds, blend together with all other Subconscious Minds and flow into the Super Conscious Mind. This mass is a hologram and each iceberg a piece of the hologram. Each contains all the information of the larger mass. And so we have the parts and we have the whole, or more poetically, "the universe in a grain of sand." Each of us is a piece. Each of us is the whole. By entering the whole through entrainment of our minds we are able to enjoy omni-perception. We are also able to manifest good works and abundance for ourselves and for others. When this has been achieved, Mastery of Life has been attained.

One way I put positive thoughts designed to lead to success and abundance into the Cosmic Mind and the Subconscious Minds of others and myself is through self-hypnotism. I'll record a tape that starts out by saying to relax and to go into a deep level of mind, a level of mind where my Subconscious Mind touches the Subconscious Mind of all others, particularly those who will benefit from what is on the tape. Then I'll continue with positive suggestions about whatever it is I want to influence and have happen. I'll conclude by saying that these suggestions have become part of me, and they have become part of all others who stand to benefit from them.

ESP

Not everyone receives intuitive insights or messages in the same way. Some hear voices. After learning I was writing a book, for example, a friend of mine, the founding partner of a large law firm, confided in me about several instances of this phenomenon that he had experienced. One took place between spring and fall semesters of law school when he was at a coming out party at a country club. The debutantes were making their bows, being presented to society as it were, but he was not paying a great deal of attention. He was standing with a group of friends talking and laughing, much more interested in joking around than in the girls dressed in white doing curtsies. Out of the blue a voice said, "Here comes the mother of your children." The tone was like, "Wake up, stupid, and look over there."

He wasn't sure whether the voice had come from inside or outside his head and said, "What?"

The voice returned with, "The mother of your children is coming." He turned to look. Taking a bow was a young woman he'd met before, but didn't know well. He had no plan or desire to get married. He thought this girl was attractive but he had no interest in her at that time. Two years later they walked down the aisle. As the voice had told him, she became the mother of his children.

The reception of extrasensory signals in the form of words, a sound or some form of language is called Psychic Hearing. It can be subtle, similar to what one hears in his mind when one talks to himself. It also can be loud and clear the way my friend experienced it.

Not very long ago people were sure that hearing disembodied voices meant that a person was crazy. That's why people who hear them, usually don't say so—unless they are crazy. But another friend, who is definitely not crazy, also receives messages from his intuition in the form of spoken words. This man was the owner of a successful advertising agency before he retired. He tells me that he consults his intuition on just about everything, takes a moment to listen, then gets an answer. He has opened a straight pipe to his Subconscious Mind.

Let me relate a story that this friend once told me. He had purchased a new sports car and had just driven it home from the dealership. The car had come straight from the dealer's garage where it had been prepped. He took a few moments to admire it. It looked absolutely terrific—shiny and new.

ESP

He and his wife were about to embark on a trip of about 250 miles and were planning to take the new car, so he pulled it into the driveway and up to the front door, turned off the engine, and loaded their suitcases. One bag had to be tied onto the luggage rack. Then, he and his wife climbed into the car. He took a moment to consult his intuition as was his custom.

He tilted his head. "Everything okay?" he silently asked. The voice for his Subconscious said, "Check the oil."

"Excuse me?" he said.

"Check the oil."

He got out and checked the oil. It barely came to the bottom of the dipstick. In other words, it was more than two quarts low. The engine would have been severely damaged had he driven it hard for more than 200 miles.

Once I glanced at a door prize ticket and knew instantly I'd won even before the numbers were read. The sensation I had was, *"winner!"* No subject, no object. This kind of sensation is called Psychic Intuition. It was experienced in the area of my solar plexus. It felt as though the string of a viola located inside me had been struck.

Another way messages are received is called Psychic Vision or clairvoyance. This is a form of ESP that expresses itself as a picture, symbol or visual impression. Traditionally, it is associated with receiving visual insights either through meditation, dreams, or psychometry—as in the case of the wedding ring given on the beach in Barbados. You are probably aware of psychics who help police by visualizing the scene of the crime or the location of the body. You may have had experiences with clairvoyance and not realized it. Have you ever had, for example, a mental image of an old friend and then received a phone call or letter from that person?

Psychic intuition, the instantaneous sense of knowing that I experienced when I won the door prize is the most common form of reception. Degrees of this exist, ranging from a fleeting snippet that occurs spontaneously, to a permanent gut-level realization, a sense of knowing that continuously flows.

Psychic intuition stimulated by meditation, walks in nature, or psychometry is the main way I stay in touch with the inner levels of mind. It has taken me years of working at it, but I've developed an almost continuous connection that gives me moment by moment guidance. The times I run into problems are the times I let down and allow my monkey mind (Conscious Mind) to take the helm. It's easy to know when

ESP

this has happened because a jab of fear, or flash of anger, accompanies the takeover. This sends up a red flag, and if I have my wits anywhere about me, I stop and count to ten. A few moments of meditation usually is enough to put the demon back in its place, but at times I know that it's best for me to break off whatever I'm up to, and wait until the next day before making any decisions.

Does all this mean a person should no longer use his Conscious Mind? Of course not. Rational logic has its place. But we need to recognize its limitations. The Conscious Mind can be compared to a computer. It can sort the data (anything you have read or experienced), cross tab, analyze and spit out an answer. Unfortunately, no matter how competent your mental computer is, the answer may not be correct because the analysis is limited to data that resides at Level Seven. You may even have erroneous information programmed in—about the boogieman, for instance. In computer language, "Garbage in, garbage out." This being the case, the Conscious Mind is limited, but this is not to say it isn't of value. I use my Conscious Mind to function on the mundane level. If I see a red light, I stop. If I see green, I go. You won't see me touch a hot stove, spit into the wind, or lick a frozen metal flagpole. A quick scan

ESP

of my Conscious Mind database is enough to decide matters such as these. And if something irrational pops up, my "Silent Observer" usually will spot it so I can take it out for examination. If it turns out to be a boogieman, I delete it.

The inner levels of mind should always be consulted on big issues because these levels aren't limited in any way. They encompass the whole and possess all knowledge down to the amount of oil in the crankcase of a particular car's engine.

How does one cultivate a relationship? Like any good relationship, it must begin with trust. As touched upon in the previous chapter, your Conscious Mind or ego must feel confident enough to allow access to the inner levels. It helps to attach your identity to the Divine. Otherwise, egos can be very skittish and nervous, the reason being that they are fearful of the possibility of their own annihilation. Because they are afraid of death, egos in general are looking for control. When they think things are getting out of control they will push fear buttons designed to cut you off from inner guidance.

As previously noted, I've minimized this by identifying with the spark of divinity within. When my body dies I know my Conscious Mind will merge back into the Subconscious part of me that existed before I was born. This happens every

ESP

night when I go to sleep. This merger does not mean that the Conscious Mind of this life will cease to exist. The positive parts will remain. These parts are the lessons I've learned in this life. Most importantly, I know that my consciousness will always exist. My consciousness is the Divine Spark.

Don't let your ego cause you to think that you are separate and alone. You are not. It only appears so because each of us experiences the world through senses received and decoded by our brain, which creates the sensation that our mind is located somewhere above and behind the eyes. Moreover, it's human nature that we judge what we experience, and this judging adds to the illusion. We analyze and categorize what we see according to our memories. In this way the ego creates a separate sense of self and the illusion we are separate. In one of my novels the hero, Rick, attempts to lead the heroine, Carol, to an understanding of this.

"Then, who am I, Rick?" Carol said.

"Underneath everything who you are is really quite simple," he answered. "But if I told you straight out, you wouldn't believe me.

"Then give it to me roundabout," she said.

He looked at her for a moment, apparently gathering his thoughts. At last he said, "Would you agree that language reflects our fundamental perceptions, and that it accurately depicts how we see reality?"

"I suppose so," she said.

"Then if I were to say, 'I'm going to my house,' that would make sense, wouldn't it?"

"Sure," she said.

"So the 'I' who refers to 'my house' is separate from the house, correct?"

"Of course."

"All right. So what does it mean when you say, 'My body feels tired today'? The 'you' who refers to 'my body' must be separate from that body, correct?"

She felt her brow furrow. "I never really thought about it," she said.

"A moment ago you agreed that language reflects our view of reality. If so, the sentence implies that you are not your body but something that has a body. Isn't that true?"

She hesitated before she said, "I suppose so."

"If you're not your body, who or what are you?"

"I'm sure you're going to say I'm a soul or a higher self."

He smiled. "But then, what does it mean if you refer to 'my soul,' or 'my higher self'? Who is this 'me' you're talking about?"

She shrugged. "So your point is, our language doesn't reflect reality, right?"

"Oh, but it does. In the truest, deepest sense you are Awareness itself. We each are a window on the world for the One Awareness that most religions call God. You see there's only One Consciousness, One Awareness, but in the physical reality we now inhabit, this Awareness has been subdivided so that it has billions of pairs of eyes. It has become compartmentalized."

Rick and Carol's exchange continued, but I'll stop here to say that once we realize that we each are aspects of the One Consciousness, it's impossible to relate to others as before. Our relationships must change and this includes our relationship to ourselves. When we think long and hard we will come to realize that this awareness is eternal. We will also come to realize that all knowledge—everything that has ever been said, thought, or written—exists in the One Consciousness. Edgar Cayce was able to tap into this knowledge, and the objective of this book is to help you to learn to do so as well.

To develop this ability, one must set aside the ego and identify instead with the Divine Core—identify with a vast, Infinite Self and in so doing discover true, limitless power. By realizing who we are, we can let go of fear and accept life and all the goodness, fulfillment and wonder it has to offer.

Now, please, please, do not get me wrong. When one goes from identifying with the tiny, ego self to identifying with the Divine, Higher Self, one doesn't then go about thinking that he or she is God. He or she identifies with God. But he or she also identifies with others. He is of the Divine. They are of the Divine. They are He. He is they. All is One. In this way a person arrives at true humility. He or she is neither better nor worse than anyone else. This person's spiritual condition is one of complete equality to all living things and to all living people.

How is it possible to look down upon another race or person when that race or person has at the core the same spark of divinity that animates each one of us? An individual must begin to view him or herself as one aspect of the whole family of humankind—each one a child of God.

And where will this inevitably lead? She will soon realize she has a role to play and a duty to use the talents and gifts she was born with, or developed in this life, for the betterment of all.

Chapter Five
Ask and Expect to Receive

As mentioned in the last chapter, your ego (conscious mind) wants control so that it can protect itself from annihilation. That's why it throws up flak and tries to cut you off from your innate ability for omni-perception. To combat this, beyond attempting to identify as closely as possible with the divinity within, I've convinced myself (my ego or Conscious Mind) that I do not and cannot have control, anyway. No matter how much I'd like to, or how hard I try, absolutely nothing is under my direct control except my thoughts. To believe otherwise is self-delusion.

Do you believe, for example, that you are in control of your children, that you can control their behavior through threats of punishment? Wait until you are out of sight. Then see how much control you have. The fact is, you must teach your children to control themselves. Trying to control others is a colossal waste of time and energy. In fact, I once read that anything a person feels he must control in reality controls him.

ESP

The twang of the viola vibrated inside me. Take this to heart and you're on your way.

Start slow and ease into your new relationship with the inner levels of mind. Tell them you are ready, that you want them to enter your life and to help guide you, that you'd like to form a partnership. You might begin by setting aside a few minutes each day. Call this your quiet time. Dedicate up to a half hour once or twice a day from now on. It can be the most productive and important period you spend each day.

Sit back and relax or lie down. Allow yourself to enter a state of consciousness that's different from what you're used to during normal waking hours. You might get a tape or two on meditation to help you relax, but for the first week or so don't meditate. Daydream. This may be enough by itself to create the conditions for insights to come through. Think of a quiet place, perhaps somewhere out in nature, where the temperature is perfect. Perhaps there's a blue sky and a gentle breeze. Allow yourself to go into a kind of trance, to drop to a deeper level of consciousness. Let your mind go wherever it takes you.

You may find that you begin identifying your true purpose and mission in life. You may discover your Dharma. Daydreams often are fantasies about who we really are or what we can be. They may be closer to the truth than what you thought was the truth until now.

Ask yourself what you would do if you could expand to your full potential? What is your bliss? (I'm not talking about your ego's desire to sit on the beach and pop a few beers, I'm talking about how you would like to be involved in life, not watch it mosey by.)

Some people have a regular quiet time without even realizing it. It might be when they exercise or jog. For me it is a walk I take, usually in the morning before I write.

No matter when or how you elect to spend time getting in touch, ask yourself, how do your fantasies connect with the circumstances into which you were born? What games did you play as a child? How did you entertain yourself? Have you any interests that go back as long as you can remember?

After your quiet time, take a few minutes to jot down thoughts and ideas that came to you. Ask yourself, are you now doing what you like? Does what you do help others in some way? With your background and training, what could you do? If you could have whatever you want, be whatever you want, what would that be? How would this help others?

ESP

Take notes each day for several days. What themes recur? Keep writing things down. A pattern will emerge. Stay with it. Develop recurring themes into a vision. Whatever this entails at first may seem impossible, but your internal naysayer may simply be your ego talking. Don't let your ego get in the way just because it is terrified. Stroke it. Tell your ego you're not going to quit your day job. Not this week, anyway. You may modify your vision as you proceed, but don't start out by watering it down because of the seemingly "practical" voice of your ego. Your inner mind already has the end result in mind. It knows. Let it help you bring this into focus.

At a deep inner level of mind, you know how your vision can be achieved. Allow yourself to be shown the way. Ask for guidance in your daily quiet time. Sometimes the information you need will come immediately. Often it will not. Ask. Be patient. An answer is on the way. It may arrive in several days, or even a week later.

Often, I'll ask a question of my inner mind at night before I go to sleep. If possible, I phrase the question so that a yes or no answer is sufficient. I conclude by saying, "When I wake up tomorrow, let me realize the best course. Give me a sense of knowing."

This almost always works.

You may be wondering, how can I tell if my inner levels of mind are guiding me or if it's some other part? It could be erroneous information placed in the unconscious part of my Conscious Mind like the existence of the boogie man. Many different feelings and conflicts are going on within an individual at any given time.

Boogieman fears are ego flak. They are monkey mind stuff. You can identify them because they almost always have a harried, frantic sense to them. Disregard this garbage. It has nothing to do with intuition. Your inner levels don't worry or know the meaning of fear. The inner levels are serene by nature. They don't judge or say you must follow the rules. They don't use the word "should." "Should" and "ought" simply aren't part of the vocabulary of intuition. Communication from the inner levels has a light feeling to it, a sense of "This is right. It fits." It floats on a current of air like the blithe spirit in Shelley's poem.

Your intuition never says you need something outside of yourself to make you happy—certainly not alcohol or drugs, or some other person, or a new car, or a mink coat. It is not the inner voice that says, "If only I could get a promotion, or win the lottery, or score a touchdown, then I'd have what I need." That's the ego talking—tapes playing that are stored in the unconscious.

The inner levels don't say these things because the inner levels know you have everything you need within you—the Kingdom of Heaven is there, for goodness sake. If a voice or feeling has a sense of urgency to it, it probably has to do with some earth-bound fear or addiction. When you are bombarded with this kind of interference, release it. Let it float away. Go under this flak. Messages from deep down have to do with what is right in the long run. If you ask for the answer to a short-term problem, you'll get an answer that will serve the long haul. You may not understand at the time why you are led in a given way, but when you look back, you will. You'll see it had to do with inner things, with what is of true value, not with what will remain forever on the physical plane.

Being guided moment to moment has become a way of life for me, but I do not expect that everyone reading this book will instantly be willing to plunge into this kind of an all-out relationship. So don't feel this is necessary. Rather, ease into it a day at a time. Try making minor decisions to test how it feels. For example, suppose you go to a party and a feeling says this is not where you want to be. Your ego may counter with, "You can't leave. What would people think?"

Leave. Go home or wherever your inner voice directs you. When you arrive, calm yourself. Check how you feel. If you were following inner guidance, you'll feel light. You'll feel more alive. You'll have energy. Remember this because in the future, even after you've made a big, life-changing decision, you'll experience this same sense of buoyancy after following direction from your intuition. If you are off course, you'll feel drained, blocked, maybe even depressed. When you experience these feelings, it's time to reconsider.

As you work at listening to and practice following these messages, you'll find they get stronger. After a time it will become easier to sort out ego-based voices from communication that stems from the inner levels. Start with matters that aren't all that important and let your confidence build. If you persevere, you will come to a point where you are willing to let your life be guided in this way.

I won't try to tell you this whole business isn't a little bit scary at first. But once you start down this path, you won't want to turn back. You'll experience a new sense of freedom.

ESP

I guarantee it will be an adventure. A hero's adventure. And you'll arrive on a higher plane of understanding.

Perhaps right now, today, you feel a sense of frustration with your life. You know something's wrong, that you'd be happier doing something else, but you don't know what. Begin consulting with your inner wisdom. Remember what James, Jesus' brother, said: "Ask." Ask to be shown the way. Keep asking if you don't get an answer right away. In matters of the inner mind, this always works. You can be confident you will get an answer, and if you run with it, that things will change. There can be no other result. Your ego self will be terrified. Tell it to hang on and trust. Your Higher Self is a gung ho type who knows no fear. It's more than willing to lead you into the unknown.

And be prepared for obstacles to arise. You almost certainly will reach a point, as I did, when you will doubt that you have made the right move. You may even doubt that such a thing as a Higher Self, and inner levels connected to the Cosmic Mind. This will happen because it is part of the script of the classic hero's journey we are all destined to take—probably several times in a single life. Read Joseph Campbell's *Hero with a Thousand Faces*. The crisis of belief faced by the hero, the period of uncertainty and doubt, has been an important element of the hero's adventure from the beginning of time. It's there to test resolve. So just keep on plugging, and eventually the invisible hands of Grace will come to your aid. You'll be guided along miraculously as the Life Force, the opposite of entropy, folds in behind to support you. As you move ahead, ask for awareness. Ask for a sense of knowing what to do next.

You might ask this at night before bed, as I often do, or during your daily quiet time. You may receive an image, a feeling, or an answer in words right on the spot. You may draw a blank. If so, go about your business, but expect an answer. Trust that an answer is on the way. This may come in a dream or it might come from outside yourself. You are part of the All, remember? Your mind and the Super Conscious Mind are one—everywhere at once. Nonlocal. The answer can come from anywhere. So be attentive.

Answers that come from outside me usually arrive in written form. A phrase or paragraph in a book I'm reading will stand out. The medium could be almost anything: a fortune cookie, a comic strip, the Bible, Dear Abby. Whatever it is will strike a chord. It will be accompanied by that sense of "knowing" and possess meaning in regards to my situation that the author may not have had in mind.

ESP

How does this work for me on a daily basis? Let's say a question or problem occurs in the morning while I'm working. When lunchtime comes and I'm out and about, I'll take a side trip to the library or a bookstore. I'll go to whatever shelf seems appropriate and take down whichever book grabs my attention. I'll open the book at random. Usually, the answer will be on the first page I turn to. If not, I'll close the book and open it again. If the answer still isn't there, I'll try another book. Seldom do I pick up more than three books.

A friend tells me his answers usually come from other people. It could be something the preacher says in a sermon on Sunday. Or my friend might be engaged in a conversation at work about something totally unrelated, and a sentence or phrase a person says will jump out at him. He has his answer. The meaning for him may have nothing to do with what the person talking was attempting to communicate.

Ask your intuition to direct you to a better life. Let it show you step by step. Don't try to force it. Don't make yourself make decisions. Just let things take place. If you allow yourself to be guided, things will happen. Remain flexible. Trust. Things probably will not occur the way you expect, nor will you end up where you thought you would at the outset. If

ESP

you travel down a path only to find a dead end, then look around for the open door. It will be there. You were led down that path because that's where the door is.

Your Higher Self knows what it's doing. It won't let you starve. At times things may look bleak, though, so be prepared. You may wonder what's taking so long. Your Higher Self seems to delight in cutting things close. The scheduling often seems just in the nick of time.

Something may happen that at first seems like a disaster. For example, you might lose your job. If so, it is part of the plan. The crisis has come so keep plugging. Don't turn back. You could turn into a pillar of salt. A much better opportunity will come along.

Chapter Six
Keys that Unlock Intuition

Hidden from view, in back of, underneath, yet giving substance and life to all things, is what you came from and are still connected to: One Spirit.

As was said many times by Edgar Cayce, "Spirit is the life, mind is the builder, and the physical is the result." This means our physical bodies are in reality projections of our minds. Your Subconscious Mind has been built up over many incarnations. It is immortal and contains everything you've ever learned, plus the information that, working in concert with genes that come from your biological parents, forms and maintains your physical body.

When the body becomes old or diseased or broken, or when we have accomplished the mission, or learned the lessons a particular life has to offer, we cast off the body and return to the Universal Subconscious Mind, or One Spirit, that is our home. There we reflect on the life just lived and internalize its lessons. When the time is right we will return to physical life through the medium of birth in order to learn new lessons.

Some of us have specific missions to accomplish in a particular life, and some of us do not. All of us will have Dharma, which is the essence of our soul and the gift we have to give others. For, as Dr. Laurel Clark, the leader of the Dharma weekend said, "Humankind is like a giant jigsaw puzzle. Each piece is an individual soul that fits perfectly into the whole. All of us are unique and possess something of value that no one else can share in precisely the way we do."

We need to use our intuition to find out what that is. Then we need to use our intuition to determine the most fruitful and productive way to share it. When that's what we are about, the One Spirit will come to our aid.

As a young adult, I toyed with the fashionable movements of the '60s, existentialism, nihilism, hedonism. I read Jean Paul Sartre and Albert Camus, but their points of view did not ring true. Where, for example, had the a priori knowledge I was born with come from? I could recall lying in a crib and wondering who I was and where I was. How could this be if the awareness I was experiencing was a phenomenon created by

ESP

nerve ends firing? How could I even know that there was such a thing as "Who one was," or "Where one was?"

As I grew up, there were plenty of other times when I'd known something with no apparent way of knowing. By the time I reached adulthood, it was clear to me I did not understand the true nature of reality, and after a while I came to the conclusion it was impossible to know. I did my best to shut the whole thing out of my mind. It seemed a much better use of my time and energy to chase women, drink beer, Scotch whisky, martinis by the dozen, and to make money so I could chase more women and drink more Scotch—the good stuff. Twelve years old at least.

My wake up call came in 1970. At the time, I lived in a hundred year old townhouse with three other young men in the Bolton Hill section of Baltimore. It was a charming section of town with wrought fences and gates, white stone steps and window boxes filled with geraniums and impatiens. The look and the feel of the neighborhood was reminiscent of Mayfair or Bloomsbury in London, and as such attracted many would-be Bohemians such as myself and my roommates. We occupied an apartment fashioned from the second and third floors at the back of a red brick mansion.

ESP

Perhaps as a consequence of too much partying and not enough sleep, which had caused my immune system to let down, I'd contracted a case of the flu and was upstairs flat on my back in my bed, sweating and staring at the ceiling on a Saturday evening in June. Downstairs, the front door opened and closed with a bang accompanied by male and female voices and laughter. As the evening drew on and darkness fell, the din from below grew into what I recognized was an all-out party. I felt weak and feverish, but by God there was a party in my apartment. So I got up, pulled on some pants and a shirt and went down to join the merriment.

In the kitchen were a dozen or so young men and women drinking everything from margaritas to screwdrivers to tequila shooters and beer. As for myself, I'd developed a taste for Scotch while in the Bahamas during spring break a few years before. It had happened after what had seemed like an hour waiting in a line five abreast and more deep at the bar of a nightclub. I'd ordered two bourbons and water instead of one so I wouldn't have to suffer the wait again for a while. But when I got back to my table I found the bartender had given me Scotch, and rather than fight that line again, I drank them both. That was enough.

ESP

In Baltimore at my apartment that evening, I spotted a nearly-full bottle of the good ship Cutty Sark and a quart of club soda on the counter by the sink and poured half and half in a water glass filled with ice. As I sipped this elixir my case of flu seemed to subside, so I poured another and made the rounds of the kitchen catching up with friends and acquaintances. Eventually I worked my way out the back door onto the second floor back porch, with its steps leading down to the walled garden. Not surprisingly this open-air platform was the hangout of smokers—not smokers of tobacco, necessarily, although surely there were those, but rather, smokers of that weed so popular back then referred to as Mary Jane, hemp, pot, or *Cannabis Sativa* to use the Latin name. As I suppose was inevitable, I was offered the business end of a corn paper cigarette filled with the stuff, and unlike a president of the United States of my generation, I inhaled. In fact, the red ember glowed bright orange out in front of my nose and grew so long that it drooped:

Afterwards, not surprisingly, I felt very strange. Of course one feels strange after one has smoked pot, but it wasn't only in that way. I'd been used to time slowing down, my senses becoming more acute, a magnified sense of smell and the munchies. A noise a block away might seem right beside me. And there was also a sense of euphoria. But that wasn't what I felt.

I felt really, really bad.

Maybe it was the Scotch. Maybe it was the pot. Oh, I'd smoked pot and consumed Scotch one after the other, but not when I had the flu. My knees felt weak. I felt nauseous. Cold sweat formed on my brow. Unsteadily, I made my way through the kitchen and the din of the party, and with a great deal of effort, I climbed the stairs.

By now it was twilight. The room was enveloped in a dull gray gloom. I collapsed on the bed, which promptly began to spin, or so it seemed. Blood drained from my face as I spun faster and farther down into a whirlpool. I felt chilled. I shook violently—involuntarily. Then I felt my inner being rush out the front of my chest in a swoosh. All at once the spinning stopped and I was at peace. I looked back at myself, or I should say, I looked down at my body on the bed. It was sprawled out, motionless, eyes shut.

How, I wondered, can my body be lying on the bed and my mind, or—what should I call it? My perception? My conscious awareness? How could the thinking part of me be hovering above? How was it possible to be out of my body?

Then the room went black.

Next thing I knew it was morning, and I was back in my body. I still had the flu but was on the way to recovery.

For a long time I wondered about that experience. I'd never heard of anything like it and knew of nowhere to turn to find out what had happened. Nor did I know of anyone I could safely tell about the experience. I was certain any rational individual would say that I'd dreamed it. They'd explain it away as a hallucination brought about by pot, alcohol and the flu. I was sure of this because if it had happened to someone else, I'd have said the same thing. But that explanation fell short. I had no doubt I'd been up on the ceiling looking down. I couldn't prove it, of course. So I kept my mouth shut.

Gradually the incident receded into memory.

It came bursting forth some years later, in 1978. I was married by then with a five-year-old daughter. The catalyst for recall was a book called *Life After Life* by Raymond Moody. It related the experiences of many who'd had what have become known as Near Death Experiences (NDEs). The author detailed the various stages beginning with the sensation of rushing out of the body, and looking back calmly to observe it, of going through a tunnel toward a bright light, of being met by loved ones or other beings of light and, of course, a panoramic review of the life to date of the individual. Although my NDE experience had included only the first couple of stages, I instantly identified with what Moody was writing about, and found his book so fascinating that, to the annoyance of my wife, I stayed up most of the night and read the whole thing.

As I drank in those words I became certain that physical reality wasn't the whole story of existence. The growing realization that I grasped only part of the picture of what life was about produced in me a powerful urge to perceive the whole. A turmoil was aroused that would not allow me to rest until I understood what human existence was all about.

That same year my daughter started kindergarten at a private school across the river from where we lived. After some months of fighting a daily traffic jam caused by the merger of a busy four-lane road onto a two-lane bridge, we sold our house and bought another one closer to the school. In connection with the move I went through and cleaned out some old family papers my mother had given me, and I came across a pamphlet about the Ancient Mystical Order Rosae Crucis (AMORC), or the Rosicrucian Order as it is widely known.

ESP

Judging from the asking price on it for joining and taking a correspondence course, the dusty old pamphlet had to be thirty years old. I hadn't yet learned about synchronicity and considered this find simply to be a happy coincidence. As I read it from cover to cover, my heart skipped a beat. Here was a group that traced its roots to ancient Egypt and claimed to have the lowdown on what life was about. The goal of the Rosicrucian Order, I learned, was for its members to achieve self-mastery, an idea and a goal that struck a cord deep within me. So I wrote a letter asking for information and mailed it to the address on the pamphlet. A few weeks later I enrolled as a novice.

The house we moved to wasn't large but it did have charm. It had been built by a childless couple of means who had spared no expense on details such as crown molding, hardwood floors, and built-in bookcases. It was set back from the road on a hill in a fine neighborhood, and having been built in 1931, it had a maid's room and bath adjacent to the kitchen. I made this my study and there spent Tuesday nights for the next two years studying weekly lessons. To my knowledge the Rosicrucian Order is still going strong, but I have no idea how their lessons are disseminated today. Then they consisted of a small, eight to ten page booklet on a particular subject.

Looking back I must say that information was doled out in what now seems very small doses. My guess is the spoon-feeding approach was used to avoid knee jerk reactions. This was smart.

Giving too much at once might have stirred up anxious egos. Tests were given periodically to put the big picture in focus. Once an exam was successfully completed, students were graduated to higher levels. I've forgotten what level I achieved, but I will tell you in as brief a way as I can what it took me twenty-four months or more to learn.

Apologies in advance to any Rosicrucian who may read this and find something that doesn't exactly fit their teachings. What I have to say may be intermingled with information I picked up from other sources, as I did not limit my studies to the Rosicrucian materials but rather read widely on the subject of metaphysics. Moreover, everything here has passed muster with the inner levels of mind, and much of it may have come directly from that source.

We humans tend to accept at face value what we see around us, and because of this we do not understand the true nature of our world. For example, we usually fail to consider that our sight is limited to a relatively narrow spectrum of light. Much is going on around us that our eyes are unequipped to see. Consider, for example, the signals from cell phones, television and radio transmissions, and light that falls outside what is visible to humans, such as the infrared variety. Moreover, our eyes can and do play tricks on us. Light strikes the retinas and this is transformed into electric impulses that travel along the optic nerve to the brain, where the signal is unscrambled. What we think we see is actually a construction of the mind arranged in a way we can understand. What's out there looks like solid stuff.

Objects appear to be separate from one another and so we come to believe that our world is made up of individual components. But quantum physicists have been telling us for some time now that what we regard as solid objects actually are made of energy. Nothing is separate. All is connected because all is energy. Things only appear separate because the atoms and molecules that form them are vibrating at different rates.

As has been noted by physicists, the whole of reality can be compared to a giant thought. One last time I will repeat the words of he great twentieth century prophet, Edgar Cayce.

"Spirit is the life, mind is the builder, and the physical is the result." He said, "Thoughts are things." One all-pervasive spirit is behind all existence. Our reality is a projection of the universal mind. This is Truth. It is the most profound understanding—the highest form of omni-perception—one can attain.

The saying "as above so below" is true. The mind of an individual produces his or her reality. Or, as the Bible verse from Proverbs says, "As a man thinketh, so is he." Whatever thoughts, ideas, desires, or fears we dwell upon will eventually come to pass because it is the job of your Subconscious Mind, working in concert with other Subconscious Minds and the Super Conscious, to fulfill them. This is how our desires sometimes appear to be miraculously fulfilled. I had the desire and intention, for example, to learn about the true nature of reality. "Coincidentally," I found a pamphlet printed thirty years prior by the Ancient Mystic Order Rosae Crucis. Once you begin to expect synchronicities such as this you will recognize them all the time and begin to rely on them as I do.

Whatever we dwell upon, including our worst fears, will come to pass in the same way. I will not go into the enormous implications of this here, except to encourage you not to let your mind focus on problems, illness, or anything else you do not want to come into your life. Rather, allow it to focus on love, abundance and prosperity, and this will be your experience.

So, what we have is One Mind we all share.

This was the realization that created in me the urge to know my Dharma and to identify my mission. As my understanding of reality grew, I came to understand that this life is not our only life, and that in this particular life I had a mission—an assignment.

I can still recall when I was a baby lying in a crib, looking up, and wondering, "Where am I? Who am I?" This memory comes as though enveloped in mist, and is accompanied by the uncomfortable sensation of being unable to rise up or turn over. My crib was positioned beneath an open window flanked by wispy white translucent curtains. The air of a gentle breeze sought entry causing a Venetian blind to tap lightly against the window frame, its slats closed against the brightness of day.

It did not seem strange to be in a crib. The room was familiar, somehow, and I struggled to remember.

"Who am I?"

What came to mind were friendly, familiar faces. They surrounded me, smiling, laughing, and offering encouragement. I know now who these friendly faces were, but it was a long time coming. They were members of my soul group bidding me, "Bon Voyage." They were waving good-bye from the second level of consciousness. "Go to it, Old Fellow," they were saying. "You can accomplish your mission. We know you can. And whenever you need help, just call on us!"

We each belong to soul groups. These are individuals on our same level of development with whom we incarnate time after time. We have banded together to aid one another in our mutual development and evolution. Our work as a soul group is not limited to the time we spend between lives. When we sleep we return to the Subconscious Mind, the One Spirit. We often meet and plan events and programs that are constructed to further our development. Soul development is our overarching purpose and mission.

As a child in a crib, however, I had no way of knowing who I was or why I was or from where I had just come. After a while I fell asleep, comforted by the friendly faces still residing in my mind's eye. I can still see them today.

Later, I awakened and felt my pulse quicken. Four faces were gathered alongside my crib, looking down. These were not the same faces. What disappointment I felt at that realization. Though unknown to me at the time, these new faces were of my brother, sister, mother and father of this lifetime. I was grown before I gained even a limited understanding of this memory, which is not surprising considering I was raised in a fairly typical family on a steady diet of ideas and perceptions held by most educated Americans of the '50s and '60s. The notion of reincarnation, for example, indeed the scheme of our existence as I now understand it, was not something we chatted about at the dinner table.

All my life it seemed as though I could perceive things, understand things, that I should not. I could see events developing sometimes so clearly that it was frightening. People said I could not do this, that no one could know the future, and I believed them. After that, whenever a premonition would come, I would dismiss it. Simply put it out of my mind as nonsense. If others could not see the whole, why should I be able to? Still my ability at perception persisted. Once I was shocked, and no doubt so was my teacher, at the score I received on a standardized test that was meant to measure abstract reasoning. It was quite literally off the chart. This did not fit the data in my teacher's Conscious Mind, however, and though she did mention it, she did not discuss the implications of it with me. Had that teacher been wise, however, she would have told me that I possessed a special ability. Had that happened, I might have put the ability to better use much earlier in life. Rather, it took until my fifties for me to begin.

Better late than never.

It is perhaps a universal urge we all share to know who we are and why we're here. If we only knew, we wouldn't waste time heading down blind alleys or getting off at wrong stations. We'd be able to direct our efforts in such a way as to live a fulfilling life. We'd be empowered to use our talents in the most productive manner. Our fellow humans would be well served, and we in turn would find contentment and peace of mind.

To know for certain my true calling has long been a personal dream of mine. Even though I've done my best to follow my heart, I hadn't felt at peace or certain that my activities have been channeled correctly. The weekend in Windyville taught me I am meant to teach. This little book presents an effort in that regard. It contains the essential basics you need to know to develop intuition, your own omni-perception.

So, let me put it all together. If you have been paying attention, you will recognize these as the keys to unlock the wisdom and knowledge of your Higher Self:

ESP

1. Beware of the human tendency toward denial. Widen the gap between stimulus and response. Be open to new, and to what may at first seem "off the wall" ideas. If you are a Republican, at least listen, truly listen to what Democrats have to say about a subject. Vice versa, if you are a Democrat. And you Egyptologists need to listen, too.

2. Identify with the Divine, not the temporal. Know that Truth cannot harm you. Know that you came from and are still connected to the One Mind. To unleash your sixth sense, you simply need to open a passageway. When all is said and done, that's really what all this is about.

3. The past is gone so put it behind you. Live in the present with an eye toward the future. Seek possibilities. Ask for truth and guidance. Be open-minded.

4. Believe in ESP and intuition. They are real and can work to your benefit and to the benefit of others. Remember to use your intuition and your skills and talents to help others and in so doing help yourself. We are all part of the human family, all children of the One Mind.

5. Entrain your mind. Be still and be patient. Entraining your mind through meditation, a walk in the woods, or other

quiet activity that for example puts you in touch with nature, will open the pathway you seek to the One Mind.

6. Learn to separate monkey-mind thoughts from psychic intuition, hearing and seeing. Remember that an intuitive voice does not scold, try to guilt-trip you, or say, "you should, or shouldn't."

7. Look for consistency. Consider whether or not things "hang together." And pay attention to your gut, your solar plexus, or the area around your heart. *Feel* what it is trying to tell you. If the facts and circumstances hang together, go with what you are feeling. It's important to make a decision. And once you have made a decision, stop and consider how you now feel about it. If the situation and the decision you made feels right, then move ahead full speed ahead. You are on the right course.

If something is telling you that you just made a mistake, start looking for an exit ramp. The One Mind will not allow you to go too far off course, if you pay attention to what it has to say.

As you practice and follow these seven keys and put them into practice, the more your relationship with, and your communications pathway to the One Mind will grow.

The author, Stephen Hawley Martin, is a former marketing executive and consultant and the author of more than three-dozen books, including five published novels, half a dozen business management titles, and quite a few self-help books and metaphysical investigations. He is a former principal of the world-renowned advertising agency, The Martin Agency, the firm that created the GEICO Gecko and "Virginia is for lovers." Today, Stephen is editor and publisher of The Oaklea Press. Listed in *Who's Who in America,* and best known as a award-winning author, Steve is the only three-time winner of the *Writer's Digest* Book Award, having won twice for fiction and once for nonfiction. He has also won First Prize for Visionary Fiction from *Independent Publisher* and First Prize for Nonfiction from *USA Book News.* He and his wife of 35 years live in central Virginia.

To get in touch with Stephen and learn about other books he has written, visit his website:

www.shmartin.com

Afterlife, The Whole Truth
Life After Death Books I & II
Stephen Hawley Martin

This two-book volume contains the bestselling title, *Life After Death, Powerful Evidence You Will Never Die* and the sequel, *Heaven, Hell & You.* As one reviewer, a medical doctor, wrote: "Extraordinary findings . . . will keep readers on the edge of their seats as they burn through this well written book's pages."

Kindle: ASIN: B07J46QQW8
Paperback: ISBN-10: 1727782038

THE THREE KEYS TO LASTING HAPPINESS
AND HOW TO OBTAIN THEM
Stephen Hawley Martin

You were born for a reason, and if you don't know the reason, you cannot be making progress toward its fulfillment—and so you likely feel that something's missing in your life. This book provides a methodology to learn why you're here, and it will hand you three keys that will open your eyes to what can bring you lasting happiness. Don't miss it.

Kindle: ASIN: B0C67MHNJF
PB: ISBN-13 : 978-1892538710

The True Holy Grail
The Secret You Can Use To Create the Life You Want
Stephen Hawley Martin

Some searching for the Grail thought it was the cup Jesus used at the Last Supper. Others, a dish, or a stone. All believed it had powers to create happiness and wealth. This book explains that the True Holy Grail is secret knowledge that enabled Jesus to work miracles. This book tells that secret.

Kindle: ASIN: B07MYQ8N8V
Paperback: ISBN-10: 1794500715

What Every Thinking Person Must Know

How Science Reveals God

Stephen Hawley Martin

Have you ever had a doubt that God exists? Stephen Hawley Martin draws upon evidence from five areas of scientific exploration to make an irrefutable case for the existence of God and the creation of the universe and life. This is a book you'll want to share with all your doubting Thomas friends.

Kindle: ASIN: B07X7FHG1H
Paperback: ISBN-10: 1687528594

Life After Death
Book Two,
Achieve Joy Now & Bliss in the Afterlife
Stephen Hawley Martin

Once you have reviewed the evidence and have beomce conviced that you are an eternal spiritual being having a temporary physical experience you will want to read the this book. In it, the author descibes what it was like to merge with the Cosmic Mind, and he shares insights he brought back with him that you can use to find joy in this life and bliss in the next.

Kindle ASIN: B09GHY3SRN
Paperback ISBN: 979-8479020360

Edgar Cayce, The Meaning of Life and What to Do about It

Stephen Hawley Martin

You may believe humans are spiritual beings having a physical experience, but are you sure why we're here and what we ought to do about it? This book will tell this you this and much, much more because, as the record shows, the accuracy of information revealed by Edgar Cayce's more than 14,000 psychic readings was nothing less than extraordinary.

Kindle: ASIN: B07L7GF3HH
Paperback: ISBN-10: 1790978114

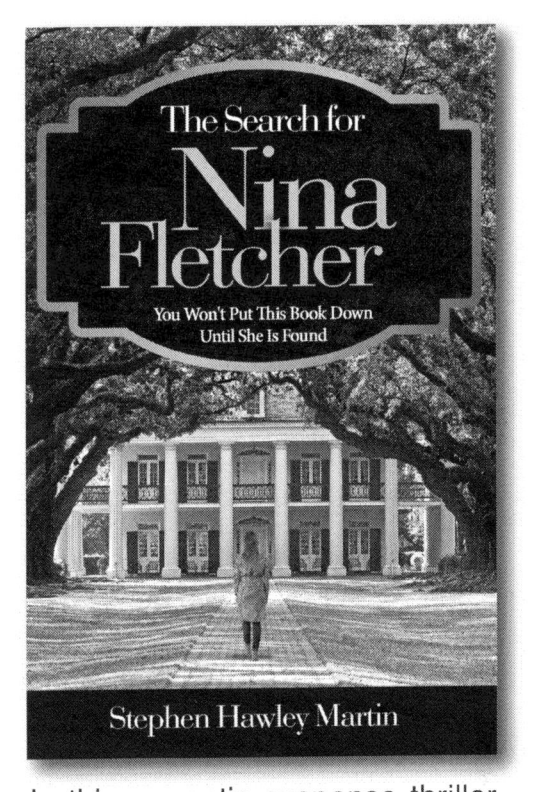

The Search for Nina Fletcher

You Won't Put This Book Down Until She Is Found

Stephen Hawley Martin

In this romantic suspense thriller, Rebecca wants to save the beautiful plantation home where she grew up, but to do so she must find her mother. If only she could remember what happened in the basement of the old house in Baltimore long ago. She must find out what happened there, she must!

Kindle: ASIN: B01J6MQZXS
Paperback: ISBN-10: 1535580879

Death in Advertising

FICTION FIRST PRIZE WINNER — WRITER'S DIGEST

Stephen Hawley Martin

This whodunit set in an ad agency won First Prize for Fiction from *Writer's Digest* magazine. According to Mike Chapman, Editor-in-Chief of *ADWEEK* magazine, this novel is "A thrilling and evocative read. Masterful attention to detail brings the ad agency world to life and delivers a gripping whodunit." Get ready. You won't be able to put it down.

Kindle: ASIN: B00UIGGKUA
Paperback: ISBN-10: 1511662921

THE SECRET OF Life

An Adventure Out of Body, Into Mind

Stephen Hawley Martin

Visionary Fiction WINNER — Independent Publisher

Romantic suspense at its best, this fast-paced novel won First Prize for Fiction from *Writer's Digest* and First Place for Visionary Fiction from *Independent Publisher* for good reason: It's very hard to put down. You'll be riveted as Claire flies to the island of Martinique to solve a mystery and soon realizes she's being stalked by a drug lord.

Kindle: ASIN: B08S7MG4WM
PB: ISBN: 979-8591416515

Made in the USA
Columbia, SC
13 October 2023